World Culture Districts

Spaces of the 21st century

Editor: MQ, Christian Strasser

Content

Cultural Districts, Utopias, and the Global Society

by Christian Strasser

Cultural districts are the flagships of an internationally connected world. On the one hand, their orientation and networks are global; on the other, they are perfectly anchored in their local and regional scenes.

Cultural districts are often defined as so-called "third places", a term coined by the sociologist Ray Oldenburg to refer to neutral ground that is in principle open and easily accessible to all social levels; where communication is welcomed and a pleasant, playful atmosphere reigns; and which is visited regularly by visitors who see it as a kind of public living room (Oldenburg 1999). Oldenburg considers such places to be highly socially relevant, for they offer open space in which to linger and thus are used intensely by different communities. Cafés and libraries are also "third places". Cultural districts represent a special category, however, because they are largely consumption-free zones with no commercial agenda. Their central concern is the communication of art, culture, and knowledge. The world has changed significantly within a very short time due to the Covid-19 pandemic. Following an initial period of uncertainty, it turned out that cultural districts are more flexible entities than had been assumed, and even in times of crisis are able to fulfil a supporting social function. Even if they cannot be active in their every part, their open spaces can continue to be used meaningfully under different conditions. In this sense, it can be said that cultural districts are able to cope very well with serious crises of this kind thanks to their multidisciplinary and multilayered nature, their programmatic variety, and the orientation and diversity of their players.

← Royal Museum in Berlin, 1832, Johann Heinrich Hintze (1800–1861)
Photo © Märkisches Museum, Berlin

← Centre Pompidou in Paris
Photo © Gabriel de Andrade Fernandes, Wikimedia Commons, CC BY-SA 3.0

→ MuseumsQuartier Wien, Main Courtyard
Photo © Hertha Hurnaus

From Museum to Cultural District

Cultural districts are often to be found in important and vibrant areas with a long and significant past. When considering their development and growing importance, it is worth examining this historical background.

Museums emerged in the nineteenth century as educational institutions of the middle classes. Historian Jürgen Osterhammel includes them, along with archives and libraries, among what he terms "places of memory", in which "the past is preserved in the aggregate of possibility"[1]. While such places had already existed in previous centuries, in the nineteenth century their importance for a growing general public increased. Borrowing from ancient terms such as "aula" or "agora"—places of assembly—these new institutions were intended to educate and impart knowledge through the dissemination of art history, cultural comparison, and an exchange of ideas.

While initially starting from this universal claim, museums soon diversified, becoming places of education specialized in different artistic epochs and scientific disciplines. In the sciences, too, more and more diverse subjects gradually emerged. The modern world was oriented toward constant human progress. In art, the avant-garde sought to break with tradition and introduce new techniques, content, and perspectives, claiming to represent a new and valid state of artistic development. In the twentieth century—"the age of extremes", to quote the historian Eric Hobsbawm (Hobsbawm 1994)—and with the impact of the world wars, the arts splintered further. The avant-garde was followed in the postwar years by postmodernism and with it a pluralism of artistic forms, media, and modes of expression. Artists began to expand the classic fields of art production and presentation, to self-organize, and to claim new spaces for their art. At the beginning of the twenty-first century, alongside art institutions and commercial galleries, artist-run spaces emerged, which, in combination with studios and a growing creative economy, revitalized and redefined entire city districts.

Culture as a Location Factor

As mobility increased in the second half of the twentieth century, culture also played an increasingly important role with regard to tourism. The promise of the Bilbao effect—of redefining an entire region through cultural buildings—led to a shift in thinking in many places. Moreover, in urban planning at the turn of the millennium, culture was seen as playing a key role in raising the standard of living in cities, in reallocating and repurposing land, and in creating public spaces accessible to all segments of the population. In many places, museums, theaters, and concert halls were grouped into cultural clusters, supplemented by new buildings, and made more accessible through urban planning. In many cases, old buildings have been repurposed for cultural use and architecturally reconceptualized.

In urban research, the provision of public cultural services is considered an important factor in a city's quality of life and an essential parameter of location competition. In this context, cultural districts make an unparalleled contribution to quality of life. The cultural climate and knowledge economy are decisive factors in determining an area's attractiveness, since a lively cultural life also contributes to the qualification of potential and existing employees. Creative people are drawn to an attractive cultural and creative infrastructure because they prefer places where highly qualified people already live and where there is a tolerant, cosmopolitan, and inspiring environment.

The emergence of cultural districts and their environs should not be equated with the negatively loaded term gentrification. The accusation that, in terms of urban planning, artists are utilized as pioneers to upvalue living space cannot be levelled at cultural districts, since these always represent a broad mix of different artistic and cultural approaches in both high cultural and subcultural contexts, and offer useable, commerce-free open spaces for all parts of the population.

↑ New York's High Line
Photo © Erwin Uhrmann

← Gorky Park, Moscow
Photo © Gorky Park

The Dawn of the Cultural District Era

Now, at the beginning of the twenty-first century, the era of the cultural district has begun. This is a development of global proportions, taking shape in different forms in all parts of the world. Almost all of the new districts are forming or being created in important and vibrant areas in the urban environment, most commonly in places that possess a long history. The MuseumsQuartier Wien, for example, developed within a building complex dating from the Baroque. The former Imperial Court Stables, which lost their original function following the First World War, for many years were used as exhibition grounds. It was only in the 1980s that they came into focus with a view to purely cultural use. In the midst of a dense network of cultural institutions in Vienna, the MuseumsQuartier Wien is a place of contemporary creativity, but also a place for recreation and a magnet for artists. The Quartier des Spectacles in Montréal, on the other hand, occupies an entire district of the city, where, over the course of the twentieth century, the cultural density increased until it was decided at the turn of the millennium to define the entire city center as a cultural district, and to drive future developments in this respect. Moscow's Gorky Park is a public and recreational park that was revitalized and repurposed in 2011. It is also home to the largest private collection of contemporary art in Russia. The Centre Pompidou in Paris is not only an architectural icon and museum, but a key attraction in the city for locals and tourists alike. New York's High Line, a former railway line, has become a prime example of the successful repurposing of old land. The High Line has now not only become a best practice example of the creative repurposing of an urban relic into a cultural recreational area, but also the key to a far-reaching urban development whose cultural gravitational pull has attracted a museum, galleries, eateries, residential buildings, and much more.

Cultural districts are difficult to subsume under a single denominator. They vary with regard to architecture, use, organizational structure, governance, and funding—from public to mixed funding, from community to private funding. What they have in common, however, is that they are anchored in contemporary life and creation, that they are used in a variety of ways by a variety of groups, and that they command a both regular and interested international audience. As a rule, they serve not only as places for the presentation of art and culture, but also as living spaces in which to spend time, as places of communication and discourse with far-reaching impact, and, in many cases, as creative spaces for artists.

The ever stronger exchange between cultural districts—a result of their extensive networking—takes many forms. Knowledge is shared intensively in the exchange of best practices, especially in the founding phases of cultural districts. Initiatives such as the Global Cultural Districts Network also provide a growing platform for knowledge sharing.

← "Tower Fish Pigeon" by METASITU, Alserkal Residency, part of Alserkal Arts Foundation, February 2019
Photo © Jandri Angelo Aguilar

→ "Alley of Light"
Photo © LAC 2019/Studio Pagi

The Utopian Potential of Cultural Districts

The early twenty-first century has been shaken by economic, political, and ecological crises. Dystopian visions of the future abound. For the French anthropologist Marc Augé, the problem is that people are no longer daring to imagine the future because it has already caught up with them in the form of digitalization, technologization, globalization, and all the negative ecological consequences of the industrial age. The twentieth century did not lead to the end of history, as the political scientist Francis Fukuyama predicted in the 1990s, but, as an age of warring ideologies, left behind many unsolved problems. The present is marked by uncertainties on every level. Worse than economic and political crises, however, is the Damoclean sword of impending climate catastrophe. The global Fridays for Future movement demonstrates impressively that the younger generations are refusing to accept the continuation of a global economic system based on exploitation of resources that has existed since the beginning of the industrial age. That the solution is not a simple one is attested to by science, which provides data as evidence of the climate change that is already noticeable worldwide, warning of irreversible scenarios, such as a climatic tipping effect, that will have catastrophic consequences. In his book "Losing Earth", journalist Nathaniel Rich describes the history of failures since the mid-twentieth century that have led to this point and, accordingly, offers a gloomy outlook on the future. His is by no means a lone voice. There will be no future in which ecology and sustainability are not inherently cross-sectional themes.

The solution seems to lie only in a thrust reversal that would bring about new global rules to the game. There have been very few positive approaches in this direction. Nevertheless, journalist Eric Holthaus has pulled the useful threads together and sketches a vision of what a future worth living could look like. For him, the key is a vigilant society. Augé also envisions a global society for the future,

a knowledge-based society in which nationalism and inequality are overcome (Augé 2019). But where are the conditions for such a society negotiated? From where does it receive its stimulus? Where and in which places could constructive ideas for the future take root?

The historian Jörn Rüsen describes a threefold function of culture that lies in interpretation, critique, and utopia (Rüsen 2006). This implies some of the crucial, fundamental questions that an increasingly global society must ask itself today: who are we? What has gone wrong? How do we want to live? And what do we have to do about it?

In order for cultural districts to become places where the conditions and ideas for the future can be discussed, negotiated, adopted, disseminated, and constantly re-examined, they must perform both an active and a passive role.

The passive role is to offer truly free spaces that can be embraced and used by different segments of the population. Here it is important to achieve a balance and ensure that all people feel involved and welcome. In times of globalization and migration, the importance of free spaces in the middle of urban societies increases enormously. These are places where people who otherwise would not cross each other's paths meet. These places offer individual latitude and are indeed purpose-free; however, they are also shaped by art and filled with cultural offerings. In the best case, this setting will always produce thought-provoking stimuli that pose social questions and trigger discussions. This in itself leads to an active role of cultural districts.

If one understands cultural districts as the forums of the present, then their active role comprises creating universally accessible cultural offerings and undertaking educational work to make a global knowledge-based society possible. When cultural districts address current issues, make new ideas visible, and promote an open, democratic discourse, they generate an equitable exchange between society, art, and science. If they create fertile ground for a creative economy that is driven by collaboration and synergy, and which takes account of fundamental ethical questions, then the link between art and society is also secured. Even if cultural districts are organized and managed differently, they must still foster a pluralism of ideas. Most cultural districts already fulfil these two conditions because they are supported by different communities—and so have a high level of diversity—and thus create the basis for utopian thinking and new ideas.

Access, Openness, Flexibility

An essential characteristic of cultural districts is the absence of the so-called "threshold", which often defined the entrance to an institution and in many cases manifested itself in architectural terms in the form of a high staircase. Accessibility plays a key role in the design of cultural districts. Access must be possible and attractive for all people, not only in the real world, but increasingly also in the digital world. Digitalization is written into the DNA of most cultural districts. Many already operate to a major extent in the digital world and allow users to move seamlessly between both spheres. Increasingly, digital offerings are emerging beyond the bounds of classic information. Cultural districts are flexible places. Change is a part of their constitution, which as a rule no longer follows fixed concepts of representation, but instead interacts with social change. They can be directly impacted and changed by current social and artistic developments and trends. This is particularly visible in new cultural districts, whose architecture allows the most flexible multidisciplinary use of space. In addition to interacting with the programmatic actors within, a cultural district interacts especially with its users, in a content-related exchange.

As new forums, cultural districts are arenas for social change. They offer free and open space, and they have no constraints. They are frequented by the young and socially engaged, but equally attract a culture-loving middle class and offer recreational space for parents, children, and the elderly. There are no other places where so many different sections of the population meet so informally and without reservation. This reveals the major utopian potential of cultural districts. To return to the "third place": in cultural districts, the boundaries between public and private are, to some extent, suspended. Locals mix with tourists in these spaces; they are relevant and interesting for both groups.

In societies where one hears the word "division" again and again, cultural districts provide gathering places for people of different backgrounds and views. They are neutral zones, embraced equally by all. As a consequence, this acceptance relates to the context of art and culture—for art and culture are the social glue of a global society.

"Five Artists: Sites Encountered" exhibition—M+, West Kowloon Cultural District
Photo © Courtesy of the West Kowloon Cultural District Authority

The open nature of cultural districts allows them to react flexibly to or anticipate current developments. A cultural district is never a traditionally organized administrative apparatus, but always rather the sum of individual parts, different players, and its users. Cultural districts play a crucial role in defining the broad global field of culture. They will be essential stimuli for future global development, for they represent a new, discourse-oriented understanding of society, in which the urgent questions are addressed together by all. In this respect they are already the venues of the future. Cultural districts are the bedrock of hope for the twenty-first century.

Further reading

Marc Augé, "Die Zukunft der Erdbewohner. Ein Manifest", transl. Daniel Fastner, Berlin 2019.

Francis Fukuyama, "The End of History and the Last Man", New York 2006.

Eric Hobsbawm, "The Age of Extremes", London 1994.

Eric Holthaus, "The Future Earth: A Radical Vision for What's Possible in the Age of Warming", New York 2020.

Ray Oldenburg, "The Great Good Place. Cafés, Coffee Shops, Bookstores, Bars, Hair Salons, and other Hangouts at the Heart Community, Cambridge", MA 1999.

Jürgen Osterhammel, "Die Verwandlung der Welt. Eine Geschichte des 19. Jahrhunderts", Munich 2016.

Nathaniel Rich, "Losing Earth: The Decade We Could Have Stopped Climate Change", New York 2019.

Jörn Rüsen, "Kultur macht Sinn. Orientierung zwischen Gestern und Morgen", Weimar 2006.

1 Jürgen Osterhammel, "Die Verwandlung der Welt. Eine Geschichte des 19. Jahrhunderts", Munich 2016, p. 31.

Alserkal Avenue

From Industrial District to a Collaborative Creative Scene

by Erwin Uhrmann

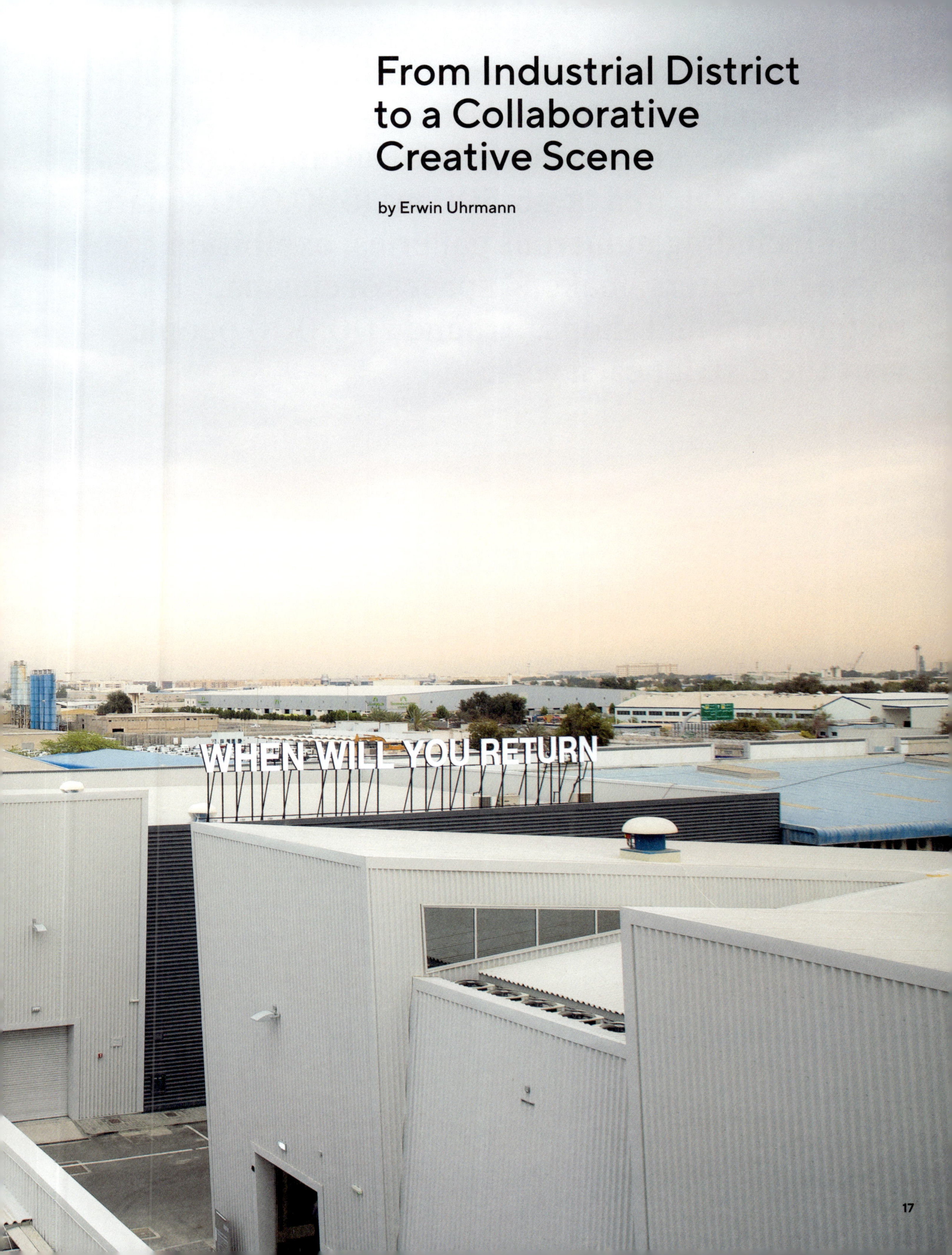

Alserkal Avenue lies some 12 km from Dubai's city center. The cultural district opened in 2008. More than seventy independent cultural players occupy a total area of 46,500 m² (500,000 square feet), including numerous galleries, exhibition spaces, theaters, makers' spaces, a cinema, restaurants, and shops. Around 700,000 people visit the district each year.

Location	United Arab Emirates, Dubai, Al Quoz 1/located in the industrial area of Al Quoz, city center
Opened	2007, the first gallery opened in 2008, extension in 2015
Total area	approx. 46,451 m² (ca. 500,000 square feet)
Number of cultural institutions	more than 60 autonomous cultural institutions and creative businesses, including a dozen contemporary art galleries and Alserkal Arts Foundation
Leisure facilities & activities	cafés/restaurants, art house cinema, blackbox theater, unisex hair salon, boutique fitness concept, yoga studio, ceramic studio, and art classes
Visitors/year	approx. 700,000
Architecture	the art galleries and cultural spaces are mainly housed in former warehouses, architectural buildings of note include reimagined former warehouses: Concrete (OMA—Office for Metropolitan Architecture), Alserkal Arts Foundation (architecture collective "a hypothetical office")
Website	www.alserkal.online

History

Beginning in the 2000s, the United Arab Emirates initiated a reorientation of its economy, culture, ecology, and tourism with a series of substantial investments, infrastructural measures, and large-scale projects. The largest cultural project under development in the region is on Sa'adiyat Island in Abu Dhabi, for which international star architects have designed several museums and cultural institutions, including the Louvre Abu Dhabi, which opened in 2017. The Sharjah Biennial for contemporary art has been held in the neighboring emirate of Sharjah since 1993. Art Dubai, held annually in the Jumeirah district since 2007, has developed into the leading contemporary art fair in the Middle East, North Africa, and South Asia.

Alserkal Avenue was founded in the Al Quoz industrial region by the Emirati entrepreneur and philanthropist Abdelmonem Bin Eisa Alserkal. One of Dubai's most influential families, the Alserkals played a significant role in the development of Dubai's infrastructure both before and after the formation of the United Arab Emirates in 1971. The family has a rich tradition of supporting the arts and culture.

↑ An Emirati woman stands inside Alserkal Avenue
Photo © Seeing Things

↖ Previous double page: Mary Ellen Carroll, The Circle Game, 2016
Commissioned by Alserkal
Photo © Alserkal

← Alserkal Avenue during Quoz Arts Fest

↘ The Third Line gallery in Alserkal Avenue

Photos © Jandri Angelo Aguilor

↓ Alserkal Avenue

Photo © Alserkal

Al Quoz's sprawling complex of low warehouses and factories forms a stark contrast to Dubai's city center, which is dense with tall skyscrapers. The 4.5-hectare site in Al Quoz is part of the Nasser Bin Abullatif Establishment, which has been owned by the Alserkal family for over seventy years. The grounds were originally used for industrial purposes, such as marble production. The redevelopment into a cultural district aimed to revitalize Dubai as a home for contemporary art and the gallery scene, and to promote art and culture to local publics and audiences. In this regard, the gallery districts of cities such as New York and London served as models for Abdelmonem Bin Eisa Alserkal, who had already been involved with several international art institutions.

Initially, thirty-nine warehouses on the Alserkal family's land in Al Quoz were converted into spaces that could be used for cultural purposes. The first to move into one of the warehouses was Ayyam Gallery in 2008. Thanks to the subsidized rent and large amount of space available—but also because of the synergies within the creative economy and public appeal—the area became increasingly attractive for gallery owners. With the relocation from Dubai's Marina district to Alserkal Avenue of the renowned Carbon 12 Gallery, founded by the Viennese gallerists Nadine Knotzer and Kourosh Nouri, the development soon gained momentum and grew both rapidly and organically. Since then, the arts scene has gradually relocated to Al Quoz from other districts. Alserkal Avenue now hosts the highest concentration of galleries in the entire region.

In response to this growth and increasing demand, plans for the expansion of the site were unveiled in 2013. The size of the original area was doubled, and sixty-two new spaces were created within the warehouse structure. The architectural firm Office for Metropolitan Architecture

(OMA), founded by Dutch architect and Pritzker Prize winner Rem Koolhaas, developed plans for Concrete, a multi-disciplinary space designed with museum-grade exhibitions in mind; Concrete opened its doors in 2017.

The not-for-profit Alserkal Arts Foundation, which functions as the engine driving the district's programming, also broadened its activities. It created an artist-in-residence program, began to focus on the region's growing artistic community, commissioned new works, and established research grants and learning and outreach programs that take place throughout the year. With such initiatives, a thriving, region-specific community of over seventy contemporary art galleries, visual and performing arts organizations, designers, and entrepreneur-led businesses has developed at Alserkal Avenue, providing an essential platform for the development of creative industries in the region.

Architecture

From the outset, retaining the original warehouse structure of the industrial quarter and converting the warehouses into cultural spaces was part of the spatial planning concept. Accents are set by two buildings that have been adapted to the spatial conditions, the area's industrial character, and flexible use. The Emirati architectural firm A Hypothetical Office designed the centrally positioned Alserkal Arts Foundation building, which with an area of 550 m² (6,000 square feet) provides studio spaces for artists-in-residence and integrates into the warehouse structure.

As part of Alserkal Avenue's expansion in 2015, a new multi-functional building, Concrete, was constructed, which together with the adjacent square The Yard represents the district's heart. The design was developed by the Dutch architectural firm OMA, led by architect Rem Koolhaas. For Concrete, the architects were formally guided by the existing appearance and flexible functionality of the district's predominantly industrial architecture. They were commissioned to transform four warehouses into one larger building that stands out with its materials of shotcrete and polycarbonate. The interior has a neutral design. Four walls, each 8 m high, can be moved to adapt the space for various purposes, such as museum exhibitions, performances, design and fashion events, or conferences. The building, opened in 2017, was one of twenty sites shortlisted for the Aga Khan Award for Architecture in 2019.

↑ "While We Wait", commissioned by the Victoria and Albert Museum, London, on show in Concrete, Alserkal Avenue from 6-18 November 2017

→ "Fabric(ated) Fractures", a collaboration between the Samdani Art Foundation and Alserkal, on show in Concrete, Alserkal Avenue from 9-30 March 2019

Photos © Musthafa Aboobacker

← Alserkal Avenue

Photo © Alserkal

Structure

Alserkal Avenue is publicly accessible, with several entrances and both indoor and outdoor spaces. The underlying industrial structure was retained, and the storage warehouses converted into cultural spaces. The site is divided into seven different thematic sectors: Art and Design, Business Services, Culinary, Lifestyle, Entertainment, Wellness, and Non-Profit. Individual galleries, restaurants, organizations, artists' spaces, cultural institutions, and shops are intermingled and reflect the organic growth of the district.

Situated between the warehouses is The Yard, a public square and the district's heart. It has frequently been used as a site for Alserkal Arts Foundation's annual public art commissions, and has been a key venue for events such as Quoz Arts Fest and the Yard Sessions. A4 Space by Alserkal, a co-working space and café, has been the birthplace of many a creative startup. Directly adjacent to The Yard is the multi-disciplinary building Concrete, which the Alserkal Arts Foundation uses as a program venue. The Alserkal Arts Foundation's offices are next door to Concrete; here the Foundation's artists-in-residence have their studios, and researchers, academics, and cultural practitioners are invited to find space to share and develop their research and practice across disciplines.

Organization

Alserkal Avenue is administered by Alserkal, a socially responsible and forward-thinking cultural enterprise established by Abdelmonem Bin Eisa Alserkal. Alserkal is dedicated to developing sustainable models for homegrown initiatives and to supporting narratives and research emerging from the Global South. Program and arts funding activities are managed by the Alserkal Arts Foundation, a non-profit that supports socially engaged and multi-disciplinary approaches and seeks to incubate creative thinking that contributes to the region's cultural sphere, leading to new forms of knowledge. In these pursuits, the Alserkal Arts Foundation awards public art commissions, operates an artist-in-residence program, funds research, and develops arts and cultural outreach programs. These activities are complemented by alserkal.online, a dynamic and holistic platform for creative and cultural discourse. Alserkal.online features content on culture, style, expression, and opinion, driving forward thoughtful discourse in the areas of food, music, cinema, art, and social responsibility, in addition to digital commissions by artists and cultural practitioners. Sustainability is a core theme of the district, attested by programs to eliminate single-use plastics, enforce waste management, and install solar panels in the Avenue.

↑ Contemporary art galleries in Alserkal Avenue
Photo © Alserkal

→ A visitor to Quoz Arts Fest in Alserkal Avenue

↖ Performance at the opening of "Fabric(ated) Fractures", a collaboration between the Samdani Art Foundation and Alserkal, on show in Concrete, Alserkal Avenue from 9–30 March 2019

Photos © Jandri Angelo Aguilor

Programming

The site's individual cultural players provide a variety of programs in their respective artistic disciplines. At the same time, the Alserkal Arts Foundation has introduced a comprehensive platform for public art commissions, exhibitions, performances, films, talks, and workshops, which stimulates dialogue between the various artistic disciplines. To this end, the main area of focus changes each year. The 2017 program dealt with the state of the arts in Dubai, questioning the conditions, mechanisms, and forms of artistic work and how they interact with other segments of society.

For larger events, the synergies and spaces on the site are used. The public square, The Yard, serves as the hub for these activities. All of the site's players collaborate to put together a program for Quoz Arts Fest, Alserkal Art Week, and November Art Week.

← An outdoor film screening in The Yard in Alserkal Avenue
Photo © Alserkal

→ Visitors to Alserkal Avenue
Photo © Jandri Angelo Aguilor

The artist commissions awarded by the Alserkal Arts Foundation make a significant impact on the district. They usually deal with topics relevant to the region and encourage collaborative and participatory approaches. One example is a group commission curated in 2019 by the artist collective 3137 based in Athens, Greece, which was also invited to participate in the artist-in-residence program. Another was the "Warehouse Project" by Dubai-based artist Vikram Divecha, in which he directly addressed the site's industrial character by collaborating with a commercial trading company. Using one of the site's warehouses as a temporary space, the company's products and activities were exhibited in an artistic setting. And Farah Al Qasimi, who lives between Dubai and the U.S., explored through photography, performances, and video the invisible work of women in production and consumption processes. A range of other artist commissions have been fulfilled by the Istanbul-based Hale Tenger and the American conceptual artist Mary Ellen Carroll, among many other international artists.

The centrally located, multi-disciplinary space Concrete serves, among other purposes, as a venue for exhibitions that are also developed in collaboration with international cultural institutions such as the Victoria & Albert Museum (London), Hayward Gallery (London), Samdani Art Foundation (Dhaka, Bangladesh) and Whitechapel Gallery (London). The space opened in 2017 with the group exhibition "Syria: Into the Light", which featured works from the Atassi Foundation's collection of modern and contemporary art from Syria.

The artist-in-residence program is a hub for both regional and international artistic exchange, focusing on research-based and socially engaged practices. Its program is divided into three cycles per year. Artists, architects, curators, economists, environmentalists, urbanists, authors, and researchers from across the spectrum of the social sciences are invited to take part. Up to four residents per cycle work in the centrally located Alserkal Arts Foundation building. Here they have the opportunity to develop new ideas and actively participate in the district's public programs. While the spring and autumn cycles focus on artists nominated by an international selection committee, the summer cycle accepts applicants via an open call.

Visitors engage with "Absolem", an Alserkal design commission by Bricklab (Abdulrahman and Turki Gazzaz) at the entrance to Alserkal Avenue
Photo © Jandri Angelo Aguilor

Impact

Alserkal Avenue has been a major presence on the international arts and culture scene since its inception, while simultaneously undergoing its own rapid yet organic growth in the region. The district and its players together with Art Dubai collectively developed and supported the region's art scene. This new art scene works collaboratively and therefore has a strong impact on the international art world. Alserkal Avenue has become the heart of the region's creative economy, with its mix of different players, many galleries, art institutions, trendy cafés, and restaurants. In addition to gallery giants like Carbon 12, the Ayyam Gallery (which has had a branch at Alserkal Avenue since 2008 and relocated its headquarters there from the Dubai International Financial Centre in 2008), The Third Line, Grey Noise, Green Art Gallery, Lawrie Shabibi, and Gallery Isabelle van den Eynde, others from international art hotspots have also opened locations in Alserkal Avenue. These include the New York-based Leila Heller Gallery and the London-based Custot Gallery. The galleries focus on contemporary art from the Middle East, North Africa, and South Asia—which has become one of the core competences of the district and the region. The galleries are active on the international art market and, as most sales take place internationally, maintain a presence at numerous major fairs worldwide.

Quoz Arts Fest 2020
Photo © Jandri Angelo Aguilor

← METASITU opening night, November 2019, Alserkal Avenue
Photo © Augustine Paredes

→ "WRECK—List of Extinct Species"—contemporary dance performance in Concrete, September 2019
Photo © Alserkal

In addition to the galleries, a number of different cultural institutions provide drawing power and a good base for the local arts and culture scene. These include The Junction, a platform for local performers, the music agency The Fridge with its own concert series on site and its focus on the Middle East's burgeoning music scene, and Cinema Akil, the first arthouse cinema in the GCC. The site is also home to star French-Tunisian artist eL Seed.

With a globally orientated artist-in-residence program and a range of artist commissions, exhibitions, and events, Alserkal Arts Foundation creates an environment that involves both local and international players. Furthermore, it supports international projects by artists from the district's galleries, pop-up projects, participation in international exhibitions, and other projects worldwide. Essential to this strategy is the district's global cultural footprint, which is achieved and is growing continually through collaborations and partnerships with arts and cultural institutions around the world.

Beyond having created and sustained this platform, Alserkal can be credited with having devised a new paradigm: a responsive business model that itself fosters new responsive business models. Sensitive to the context in which it develops, Alserkal meets the needs of local cultural and creative entrepreneurs, while providing audience-specific programming for a plurality of publics.

Gorky Park and Garage Museum of Contemporary Art

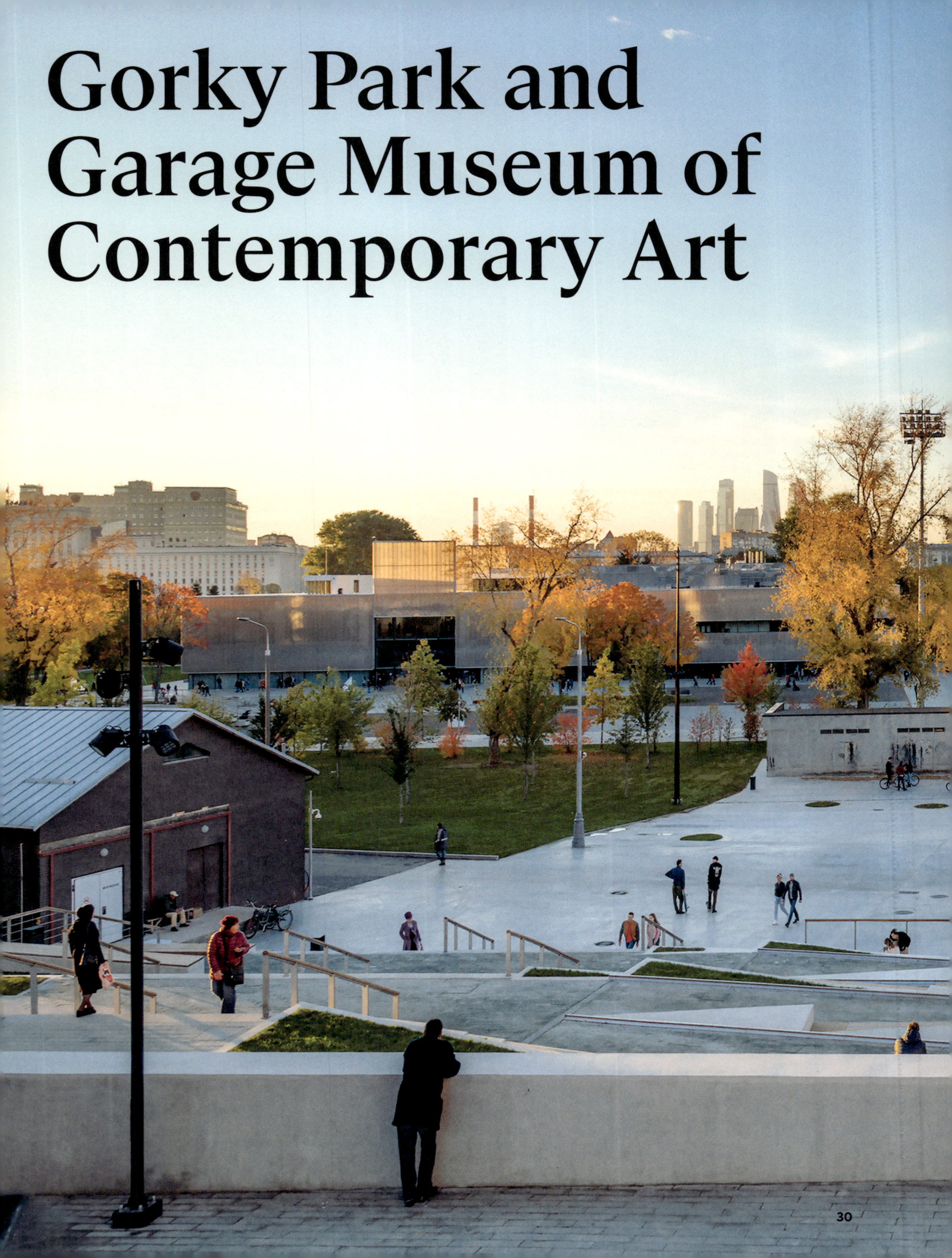

Culture and Recreation for All

by Irene Preißler

With its numerous sports and recreational facilities, Moscow's Central Park of Culture and Leisure—or simply Gorky Park—is one of the city's most-visited recreational outdoor spaces today. It is also one of the most popular places to enjoy the arts, whether by visiting museums such as the Garage Museum of Contemporary Art, attending various events and festivals, or admiring the sculptures and historic buildings dotted around the expansive park area.

Location	Russia, Moscow, Krymsky Val, 9/32/city center
Opened	Gorky Park: 1928 Garage Museum of Contemporary Art: 2008 (moved to Gorky Park in 2012)
Total area	Gorky Park: approx. 200 ha Garage Museum of Contemporary Art: 6,685 m²
Number of cultural institutions	Gorky Park: 3 Garage Museum of Contemporary Art: 2 (plus 1 temporary pavilion)
Leisure facilities & activities	public open spaces, café, museum shops, monuments, sports facilities
Visitors/year	Gorky Park: 30 million Garage Museum of Contemporary Art: 900,000
Architecture	Gorky Park/area: Alexander Vlasov, Mihail Korzhew, Vitaliy Dolganov Gorky Park/chief architects: Ivan Zholtovsky, Konstantin Melnikov, El Lissitzky, Alexander Vlasov Gorky Park/buildings: Ivan Zholtovsky, Alexey Shchusev, Yury Shchuko, Assen Spasov, Sergei Ikonnikov, Igor Vinogradsky Garage Museum of Contemporary Art/ Bakhmetevsky Bus Garage: Konstantin Melnikov, Vladimir Schukhov (1927), Yuri Grigoryan (Meganom), Jamie Fobert (2007) Garage Museum of Contemporary Art/ temporary pavilion 2012–2015: Shigeru Ban Garage Museum of Contemporary Art/ current building: Igor Vinogradsky, Igor Pyatkin (1968), Rem Kohlhaas/OMA (2015)
Website	www.park-gorkogo.com www.garagemca.org

History

The beginning of the Park's history can be traced back as far as 1000 CE, when the region was home to various Slavic settlements. Larger farms, estates, and gardens gradually emerged across the area in the eighteenth century. Count Orlov's estate was built at what would later become Neskuchny Garden; Orlov's Summer House, Bath House, bridges, and Grotto have survived to the present day. Neskuchny Garden was first to be opened to the public at the end of eighteenth century. In the mid-nineteenth century, most of the area passed into the possession of the Imperial Family and was converted into imperial premises with a palace and park facilities.

From 1890 to 1905, Neskuchny Garden was a summer residence for the Governor General of Moscow, Grand Duke Sergei Alexandrovich Romanov. Public access to the grounds was restricted. Other parts of the vast area lay fallow and therefore were chosen by Moscow City Council as the location for the municipal rubbish dump. Following the 1917 Russian Revolution, the grounds were chosen as the location for The First All-Russia Agriculture and Industrial Crafts Exhibition.

Development of the various grounds began in 1923, with the exception of Neskuchny Garden, which continued to be a recreational area for the locals. The layout of the exhibition area with its main axis and side lanes followed the flow of the Moscow River. The design defined the basic configuration for the soon-to-be Central Park of Culture and Leisure (1928), which has not changed dramatically since. Prominent architects were commissioned to design the exhibition buildings and pavilions, which were built in a range of styles and adorned with decorative paintings and reliefs. The exhibition was open from August to November 1923, and drew a total of approximately 1.5 million visitors.

Five years later, the former exhibition grounds were rearranged into the first Soviet cultural and recreational park, the Central Park of Culture and Leisure. It was opened on August 12, 1928.

In 1932, the Park was renamed Gorky Park in honor of the famous Soviet writer and major public figure Maxim Gorky. It remained open throughout World War II, displaying war trophies and serving military purposes. Many of its buildings, green spots, and the majority of its sculptural design features were destroyed during the war and were rebuilt in the 1950s.

↖ Previous double page: View of Arts Square. Entrance from Leninsky Prospekt

← View of the central part of the Park, 1930

↓ The construction of the wooden entrance to the Park at Krymsky Val in progress (from 1930). View of the Parachute Tower

→ View of the ice rink at Pionersky (Meshchansky) Pond (early 1930s)

Photos © Gorky Park

← Cascade fountain in Neskuchny Garden

→ Rotunda of the 800th anniversary of Moscow

Photos © Gorky Park

In the 1990s, the better part of the park was occupied by the Chudo-Grad entertainment complex, which transformed the area into an amusement park. Most of the historic architecture, including the many pavilions, fell into disrepair.

The reconstruction of Gorky Park commenced in the summer of 2011. All of the amusement park's facilities and rides were removed. 2,000 m^2 of pavement and 1.9 hectares of lawn and flower beds were laid. Some of the Park's sculptures were restored. Europe's largest ice-skating rink, covering an area of 18,000 m^2, opened the same winter.

The Garage Museum of Contemporary Art, which had been established back in 2008 by Dasha Zhukova and Roman Abramovich as Garage Center of Contemporary Culture (Garage CCC) at Bakhmetevsky Bus Garage in the north of Moscow, was relocated to a temporary pavilion in Gorky Park in 2012 and given its current name in 2014. Since 2015, the Museum has been housed in the building of the former famous restaurant Vremena Goda (Seasons of the Year).

In 2015, the Park History Museum was established within the Park's main Entrance Arch.

The reconstruction of the Park's historical legacy continued throughout the following years. Its infrastructure has been continuously upgraded. Today, the Park is host to various events and festivals, kids' playgrounds and rides, sports facilities and playing fields, cycle lanes and park seating.

Architecture

The principal architect of the Central Park of Culture and Leisure was Konstantin Melnikov. He designed its Parterre area, the central area of the Park, which unfortunately was not completed until after World War II, in the 1950s.

In the years following its opening, the Park had a special project office. Besides Konstantin Melnikov, its staff included the architects El Lissitzky and Alexander Vlasov.

In 1929, Lissitzky was responsible for the reconstruction of what is now the management building. Originally built in 1893 as part of Nikolai Bromley's shipyard, it was sold in 1910 and used as a factory. It was later converted into a pavilion for the First All-Russia Agriculture and Industrial Crafts Exhibition and given majolica cladding and an 18-meter-high wooden tower. Part of the building was converted into a cinema, which was designed by V. M. Voinov in association with the Brazilian architect Rodrigo Dacosta (destroyed during World War II).

Alexander Vlasov's designs included the Park's Green Theatre and Amphitheatre. He also contributed to the redesign of the grounds. The first phase consisted of the creation of five large ponds and a cascade fountain topped with a sculpture by Romuald Iodko. The water from the fountain flowed over the descending steps into the Moscow River. In 1937, Vlasov was awarded the Grand Prix at the Paris International Exhibition for his designs.

View of Fountain Square
from the viewpoint
Photo © Gorky Park

The sculptor Ivan Shadr, along with painters Alexander Deineka and Vladimir and Georgii Stenberg, was responsible for the art objects displayed in the Park.

After World War II, Vitaliy Dolganov drafted a new master plan for the entire area, taking many older designs into account. Construction of the main entrance gates began in 1955. They were designed by architects Yuri Shchyuko and Assen Spasov and consisted of an about 21-meter-high arch supported by twenty-four columns and two pylons. Two semi-circular wings were added in 1956.

The Garage Museum of Contemporary Art opened in 2008 as Garage Center of Contemporary Culture (Garage CCC) at Bakhmetevsky Bus Garage in the north of Moscow, a building designed by Konstantin Melnikov. The 1927 building is still considered a prime example of avant-garde architecture in the industrial sector. Used by Moscow's Hasidic Jewish community in the early 2000s, the building underwent extensive renovations before the Center was opened. This included the addition of 1920s-style lettering to the entrance façade and an interior design by Jamie Fobert Architects.

In 2012, Garage CCC relocated to Gorky Park, initially to a temporary pavilion created especially for the Museum by the award-winning architect Shigeru Ban, primarily known for his innovative use of natural materials. His design made use of regionally produced paper rolls for the pavilion's oval-shaped exterior front.

Exterior view of the Garage Museum of Contemporary Art
Photo © Garage Museum of Contemporary Art

↑ Mosaic inside the Garage Museum of Contemporary Art

← The Rooftop Pavilion on top of the Garage Museum of Contemporary Art

Photos © Garage Museum of Contemporary Art

In 2015, the Museum, which had been renamed Garage Museum of Contemporary Art in 2014, moved into the building of the former renowned restaurant Vremena Goda (Seasons of the Year). The redesign and reconstruction by Rem Koolhaas' architectural firm OMA retain many original features such as mosaics, tiles, and brick walls. Today the building comprises three levels with a deliberately open design. The entrance area in particular is one of the largest open spaces in the building. The front is made of double-layer polycarbonate. Particularly striking are the two large movable entrance gates, which when open allow a view from outside into the Museum's interior.

Salyut Playground is the largest open-air playground in Russia. It was opened in 2018 as a collaboration between Gorky Park and the Garage Museum of Contemporary Art to commemorate the Park's ninetieth anniversary. Nine areas containing a wide variety of materials and textures can be explored by children using all their senses. For example, the playground's Mega Swing spot consists of twenty-nine swing sets lit up in different colors at night.

To this day, renovation and reconstruction work is being carried out constantly across the grounds.

Playground Salyut
Photo © Gorky Park

Organization

The Gorky Central Park of Culture and Leisure, named after Maxim Gorky, is a City of Moscow institution under the control of the city's Department of Culture and the Moscow city administration. Gorky Park is managed by a director and has around five hundred employees. The Park is also home to independent institutions such as the Tretyakov Gallery and Garage Museum of Contemporary Art. Gorky Park is state financed; projects and festivals are co-financed by their organizers and, in some cases, by sponsors.

The Garage Museum of Contemporary Art, founded by Dasha Zhukova and Roman Abramovich, is an independent institution in Gorky Park and a private philanthropic organization in itself. Managed by a director, the Museum's income is generated through ticket sales and fundraising activities in addition to the income provided by corporate sponsors and private patrons. An endowment fund has also been in place since 2018.

Gorky Park and the Garage Museum of Contemporary Art often work in partnership. The Museum's outdoor activities, for example, are coordinated with the Gorky Park management. They also collaborate on joint projects, such the Salyut Playground.

Structure

Gorky Park is centrally located in Moscow's historic district on the outer bank of the Moscow River, between the Sadovoye Koltso (Garden Ring) and Vorobyovy Gory (Sparrow Hills). The park is open to the public 24/7 free of charge and divided into four sections: Parterre (the central part), Neskuchny Garden, Vorobyovy Gory, and Muzeon Art Park.

The Garage Museum of Contemporary Art is located in the Parterre area. In addition to the Museum, it includes the Education Center, the Garage Office, and the temporary Garage Screen summer cinema. The Garage Studios are located outside the Gorky Park grounds. The entrance area and education center are open to the public and are free of charge.

With six underground stations nearby and various bus lines running alongside it, Gorky Park is well served by Moscow public transport.

Entrance to Gorky Park from Leninsky Prospekt/Historical entrance to Garage Museum of Contemporary Art
Photos © Garage Museum of Contemporary Art

Programming

With its gardens, places to rest and relax, sports facilities, cafés, restaurants, sculptures, historic buildings, and art spread over approx. 220 ha, there is a wide range of activities for visitors to choose from.

The aim of the Park is to create spaces of culture and leisure for people in a big city center, while at the same time ensuring that the park's historical heritage is preserved. The offerings range from contemporary art to sculpture, landscape design, architecture, film, festivals, and sports and leisure activities. The park also runs comprehensive educational programs and is home to Zelenaya Shkola (Green School), a children's center.

The Garage Museum of Contemporary Art complements this program with its own comprehensive lines of exhibitions, events, educational programs, and publications on Russian and international contemporary art. The museum collection also provides the country's only publicly accessible and the world's largest collection archive of the history of Russian art from the 1950s to the present.

In addition to its exhibitions and retrospectives, the museum exhibits works produced specially for Garage Atrium and Garage Square, and explores new ways of interacting with its visitors. Each exhibition is accompanied by a diverse supporting program of lectures, workshops, discussions, screenings, artist talks, and activities for families and persons with disabilities. Garage Live features performances, music, theater, and dance events. Garage Digital connects those interested in digital-born art and AI, and the Garage Field Research program sheds light on philosophical aspects of Russian culture. The museum also

← Main Entrance Arch

→ Muzeon Park of Arts

Photos © Gorky Park

produces annual publications and houses a publicly accessible library; the Garage Journal is an independent interdisciplinary journal for the critical discussion of contemporary art; and the Garage Studios provide a total of eighteen spaces to Russian artists, where they can discuss ideas or develop new joint projects.

Gorky Park is divided into four main sections:

Muzeon Art Park, located in the northern part of the grounds, is home to more than 700 sculptures from all across Russia from both Soviet times and the present, such as the "Monument to Peter I. the Great", a 98-meter-high bronze and steel sculpture; the "Monument to Felix Dzerzhinsky" (by E. Vuchetich); "We demand peace" (by V. Mukhina); "The triumph of labor" (by M. Baburin); "Kiss" (by F. Rzaev); "Mozart" (by I. Balashov); and "God's way" (by A. Grigoriev).

Parterre is the central part of Gorky Park and contains numerous facilities. The Gorky Park Museum in the main Entrance Arch, for example, houses an anniversary exhibition on the park's first years. The 18-meter-high observation platform on its roof offers a view over the grounds. The Entrance Arch symbolizes the victory in the Great Patriotic War. Other facilities include the Garage Museum of Contemporary Art, the Orator Club Moscow for literature, a sports center, the historic Golitsynsky Garden, the Rosarium and fountain, the nineteenth-century rotundas of the former Golitsyn Hospital, a large stage for open-air events, and much more. A large skating rink is set up every winter. In 2020, the rink was themed Navigator 20°20′–20°21′ and featured recreations of various locations across Russia.

Neskuchny Garden is one of the oldest areas of the park, with many historical buildings. The oldest is the Hunting Lodge of Duke Trubetskoy. In Soviet times, it housed a tearoom; today, the popular intellectual television show What? Where? When? is filmed in the lodge. Count Orlov supposedly built the Summer House for his rendezvous with Empress Catherine the Great. There is also Count Orlov's Grotto, which used to be a popular place for lovers. Other facilities include the "Rotunda commemorating the 800th anniversary of Moscow", the Green Theatre, the Cascade Fountain, the Neskuchny Country House, and Count Orlov's Bath House.

Vorobyovy Gory (Sparrow Hills) is a nature reserve within the park, where an observation deck atop an 80-meter-high hill offers great views over Moscow. Trinity Church, which dates back to the mid-fifteenth century, and the site of N. Ogarev and A. Herzen's oath can also be found here, as well as the Luzhnetsky Metro Bridge and Vorobyovy Gory metro station (opened in 1959). At 234 m long, it remains the longest metro station in Moscow.

Impact

Originally founded as the Central Park of Culture and Leisure and later used as an amusement park, Gorky Park reclaimed its original function as part of its 2011 reconstruction, once again becoming a recreational area for people in the very center of the city. Here, one can spend one's free time in a variety of ways, whether in nature, playing sports, visiting a museum, or attending one of the many events that take place in the Park.

The Park also offers opportunities to try out new experiences, such as developing projects together with mentors as part of the "CAMPUS at Gorky Park Green School" programs. The Garage Museum of Contemporary Art offers various artistic activities and an opportunity to interact with cultural professionals. Events with contemporary artists also take place in the outdoor spaces. At the same time, the Park offers plenty of peaceful spots and spaces for retreat and relaxation.

Gorky Park with its 30 million visitors a year and Garage Museum of Contemporary Art with nearly one million per year are among the most-visited spaces in Moscow. This beautiful area with its own diverse range of art and culture, landscape design, educational offerings, and leisure activities, many of which are free of charge, offers a program that is created not only for tourists but also—and most importantly—for the people of Moscow.

← Concert at the Garage Museum of Contemporary Art

→ Visitors in the Garage Museum of Contemporary Art

↗ Entrance to the Garage Museum of Contemporary Art

Instituto Inhotim

The Pleasures of Art in a Natural Paradise

by Irene Preißler

Inhotim's location in Brumadinho, 60 km from Belo Horizonte, in the middle of Brazil, surrounded by nature, makes it a very special kind of cultural district. Nested within a large botanical garden, the center focuses not only on contemporary art, but also on nature in the form of rare plants from all over the world. Art and culture are brought closer to a broad public who also gain an awareness of nature.

Location	Brazil, Brumadinho, Rua B, 20 Fazenda Inhotim/60 km from Belo Horizonte
Opened	2006
Total area	approx. 140 ha (visiting area), 240 ha (private natural heritage reserve—Reserva Particular do Patrimônio Natural, RPPN)
Number of cultural institutions	24
Leisure facilities & activities	cafés/restaurants, design store, library, theater and education programs
Visitors/year	350,000
Architecture	galleries by Arquitetos Associados, Rizoma Arquitetura, Play Arquitetura, Rodrigo Cerviño, Paulo Orsini; landscape architecture by Pedro Nehring, Luiz Carlos Orsini
Website	www.inhotim.org.br

History

In the 1980s, the businessman Bernardo Paz acquired a farm in the Brumadinho area. A passionate lover of both art and botany, he immersed himself in contemporary art and deepened his interest in plants, especially palms.

Over the following years, Bernardo Paz continued to expand his collection. Prominent Brazilian artists such as Tunga and Cildo Meireles encouraged him to make it accessible to a wider public.

In 2002, he founded the Contemporary Art Center Inhotim (CACI) as a non-profit organization committed to the exhibiting, preservation, and creation of contemporary art. In the same year, Inhotim's first cultural facility, the Galeria True Rouge, moved onto the site with a permanent installation by the artist Tunga, soon followed by Galeria Mata, Galeria Fonte and, over the following years, by Galeria Praça and Galeria Cildo Meireles. In 2004, the center opened as the private collection of Bernardo Paz, with visits initially only possible by appointment or invitation.

↑ Aerial view of Doug Aitken's Sonic Pavilion (2009)

↖ Previous double page: aerial view of Adriana Varejão Gallery (2008) and Dominique Gonzalez-Foerster's Desert Park (2010)

Photos © Marcelo Coelho

CACI was opened to the general public in 2006. In 2010, its name was changed to Inhotim and it was officially declared a botanical garden, a designation that required not only a large variety of plant species, but also an environmental education program, scientific research, and the communication of the knowledge gained at the site.

As of 2020, Inhotim has welcomed more than three million visitors. In addition to the center's twenty-three galleries, its approximately 140-ha park is home to twenty-four open-air works of art and more than 5,000 different native and exotic plants. Inhotim currently exhibits around 560 contemporary works of art from thirty-eight countries.

Architecture

The first ideas for the site's design came from a close friend of Bernardo Paz, the well-known landscape designer Roberto Burle Marx, who acted as an advisor for the project although he was never involved in its practical implementation. His principal focus was to integrate the buildings harmoniously into the landscape and to design the gardens in such a way that they themselves would be perceived as works of art while also serving as places for relaxation.

As a tribute to Marx, Inhotim's first themed garden was named Jardim Pictórico (Pictorial Garden) in reference to the splendid colors of its plants. Areas cultivated later bear the signature of Luiz Carlos Orsini, who also incorporated ideas from the earlier gardens into his own designs. He was succeeded by Pedro Nehring, who still serves as the center's landscape architect today.

The buildings are characterized by simple forms that are integrated into the unique geography of the site and deliberately tucked away into their natural environment.

Architect Paulo Orsini designed the buildings for Inhotim's first galleries, such as Galeria Mata, whose slender lines are combined with glass, blending its interior spaces into the surroundings. The buildings were also arranged around the former farmhouse on what Inhotim's map designates as the "Yellow Route".

Following Inhotim's official opening to the public, in 2006, the district was taken in another architectural direction and expanded with a new route (the "Pink Route"), and renowned architects including Arquitetos Assocados, Rizoma Arquitetura, and Play Arquitetura were invited to build more galleries. The intention was for the buildings to enter into dialogue with the works they contained and with the nature surrounding them.

The Miguel Río Branco Gallery (architect office: Arquitetos Associados) is, at the artist's request, reminiscent of a rock standing in the middle of the forest. Its steel construction projects into the landscape in the form of a prism-shaped wedge.

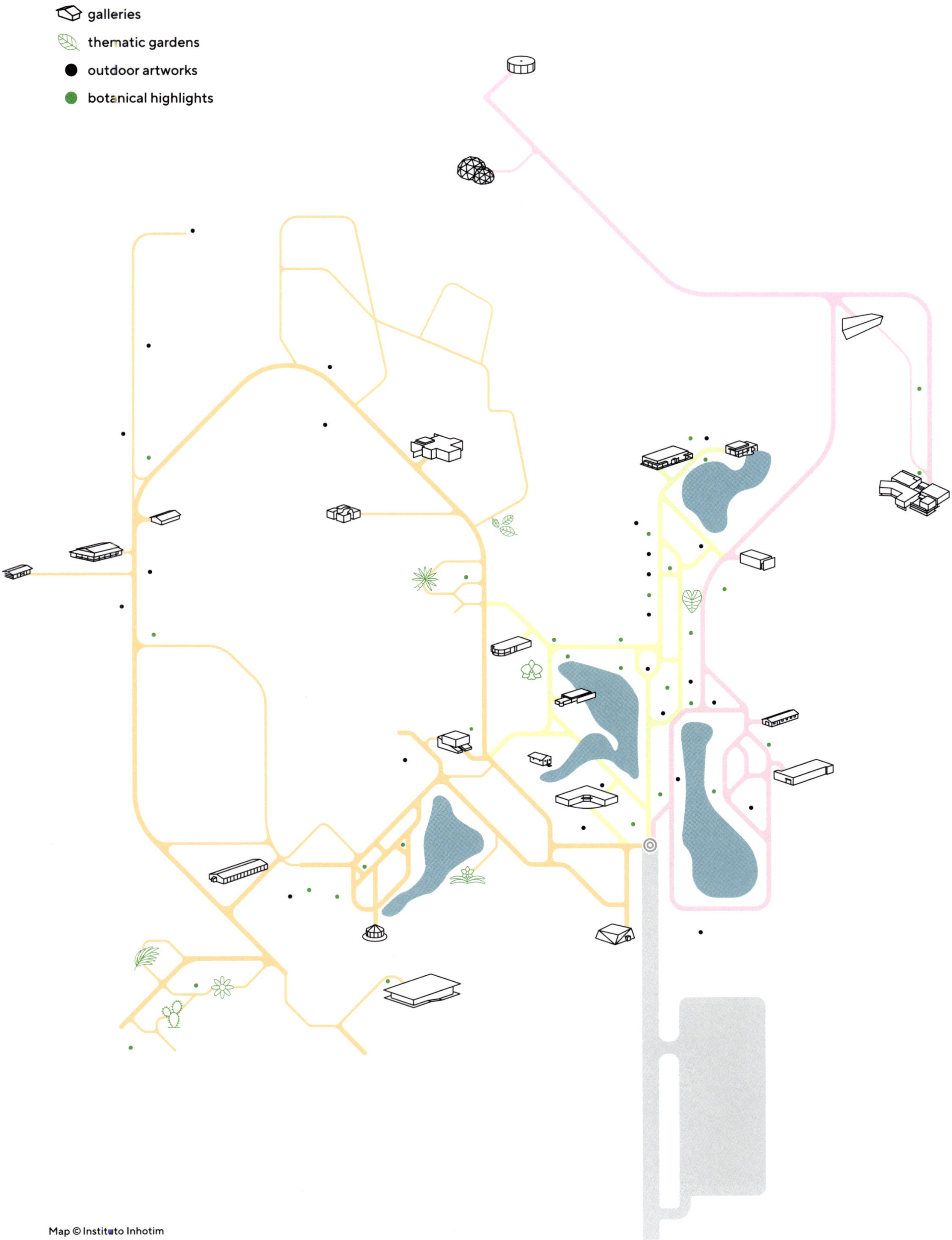

Map © Instituto Inhotim

The Lygia Pape Gallery (architect office: Rizoma Arquitetura) was built in 2012 especially for the work "Ttéia 1C". The near-complete darkness of its interior instils a sense of disorientation that contrasts with the strong sunlight outside; it also plays on the feeling of finding something hidden in the darkness. Eventually the viewer's gaze moves on towards the middle of the room and fixes on the artwork, which reflects the little amount of light present.

In order to inhibit contact with the outside world, the open structure of Marilá Dardot Gallery (architect office: Play Arquitetura)—built specially to display her work "A origem da obra de arte" (2002)—does away with walls, windows, and doors. The building is meant to serve as a temporary shelter in which the work is activated by the viewer, only becoming complete when in dialogue with nature.

Aerial view of Matthew Barney Gallery, 2009
Photo © Marcelo Coelho

↑ Rodrigo Cerviño Architect, Adriana Varejão Gallery, 2008
Photo © Eduardo Eckenfels

← Matthew Barney, De lama lâmina, 2009
Photo © William Gomes

→ Adriana Varejão, Celacanto Provoca Maremoto, 2004–08
Photo © Eduardo Eckenfels

Organization

The Inhotim Institute was established in 2002 as a non-profit organization, receiving official status as a foundation in 2004. Funding is provided through government subsidies and the Amigos do Inhotim program, through which supporters can make donations. In return, members receive discounts or special offers such as private tours led by curators. Businesses can also choose to donate a portion of their taxes to support specific projects. Additional income is generated by revenue from ticket sales, cafés and restaurants, and the Inhotim Design Shop.

The Inhotim Institute employs around 600 staff and its management is divided into four domains: the Compliance Officer, the Board of Directors, the Artistic Director, and the Botanical Garden Director, all of whom report to the Executive Board.

← Marilá Dardot, "A origem da obra de arte", 2002
Photo © Pedro Motta

→ Rizoma Arquitetura, Lygia Pape Gallery, 2012
Photo © Daniela Paoliello

Structure

Inhotim is located in the city of Brumadinho in the state of Minas Gerais. This region is characterized by its mountainous landscape and the Mata Atlântica (Atlantic Forest), a unique ecosystem that extends from the coast to the interior. It also boasts a unique type of vegetation, typical of the Cerrado, consisting of small trees and shrubs.

The entire site is divided into themed gardens, galleries, and outdoor works of art. Visitors can explore the grounds on foot or using electric mini carts, moving along various routes marked in three different colors: yellow, pink and orange.

Inhotim can be reached by public bus from Brumadinho. Private bus lines also operate between Belo Horizonte and Brumadinho or Inhotim. Entry is by ticket.

← Tunga, "True Rouge", 1997
Photo © Pedro Motta

→ Paulo Orsini Architect, True Rouge Gallery, 2001
Photo © Eduardo Eckenfels

Programming

In comparison with urban cultural districts, Inhotim is something of an outlier. With its pavilions, galleries, artworks, and installations in the open air and themed gardens, Inhotim presents contemporary art in a completely different context than is usually encountered in museums. What is more, one major focus is the experience of nature. In this setting—between gardens, lakes, and forests—one's perception of art is transformed. Many projects and works are created specifically for Inhotim's unique conditions, and so the site is in a constant state of change.

Of its twenty-three galleries, four (Lago (Lake), Fonte (Fountain), Praça (Square), and Mata (Woods)) regularly mount temporary exhibitions in which either new works are shown or items from the existing collection are recontextualized. Projects by international guest artists also feature. The duration of the temporary exhibitions varies, but their average length is around two years.

The Mata Gallery, for example, has held the exhibit "Visão Geral" (Overview) since 2019. Featuring works by the six Brazilian artists Laura Vinci, Iran do Espírito Santo, Sara Ramo, José Damasceno, Alexandre da Cunha, and Marcius Galan, the exhibition explores their different approaches to contemporary forms of sculptural production.

The other nineteen galleries present extended exhibitions of works by national and international artists. The selection is made by the curatorial team; a suitable space is then created in dialogue with the artists and architects, ultimately producing a "Gesamtkunstwerk".

Aerial view of Hélio Oiticica's Invenção da Cor, Penetrável Magic Square #5, De Luxe, 1977
Photo © Marcelo Coelho

Different genres are presented, from paintings to photography and video art, and from sculptures to installations. The Claudia Andujar Gallery exhibits more than 400 photographs of the Indigenous culture of the Yanomami; Galeria Psicoativa Tunga (Tunga's Psychoactive Gallery) features major works by that artist. Other galleries are devoted exclusively to the work of a single artist, such as Lygia Pape, Rivane Neuenschwander, Marilá Dardot, Carlos Garaicoa, Cristina Iglesias, Matthew Barney, and Doug Aitken.

In addition to the art shown in the exhibition rooms, other works are displayed in the expansive gardens, such as "untitled" (2019) by Robert Irwin. The octagonal structure made of concrete, stainless steel, and glass appears to open towards the sky like a blossoming flower. Olafur Eliasson's "Viewing machine" (2001–2008) is based on the principle of a kaleidoscope. Its overlapping reflections of light are created by six mirrors that form a hexagonal tube. "Deleite" by Tunga (1999) was one of the first works to be displayed at Inhotim. It consists of bells, sticks, chains, and iron and leather stools. "The Narcissus Garden Inhotim" is an installation by Yayoi Kusama, one of the most important Asian artists of the post-war period, and is characterized by the use of recurring motifs that refer to the artist's hallucinations.

Diversity is the dominant motif throughout the various gardens, which are dedicated primarily to preserving existing and endangered species of plants and cataloguing new ones. The collection now comprises some 5,000 different species. By presenting these rare plants and highlighting their importance for human survival, Inhotim strives to raise the awareness of nature and of the sustainable use of existing resources.

The Institute places a special focus on conveying the interaction of art and nature to children and young people in particular through an extensive educational and outreach program for schoolchildren and families. All activities take place in the Centro de Educação e Cultura Burle Marx (Burle Marx Education and Culture Center), which is open to all visitors. Other facilities include the Inhotim Theater, the Estação Educativa (Educational Station), a library, and rooms for lectures and workshops. The aim is to strengthen social interaction and to impart an appreciation for art, nature, and cultural diversity.

Impact

Inhotim is located in the middle of Brazil, in the state of Minas Gerais. The area is known for agriculture and mining; cultural activities generally take place in large cities. Inhotim thus plays a major role in positioning art and culture away from the big metropolises.

To promote social and cultural exchange, a variety of activities are developed annually in partnership with the city of Brumadinho. One such initiative, started in 2019, is the Nosso Inhotim campaign, through which Brumadinho residents are given free admission to Inhotim and discounts for the events taking place there.

A further initiative to promote local cultural forms of expression is Palco Brumadinho (Brumadinho Stage), which was developed in 2019 together with Brumadinho-based artists. Events featuring traditional singers from the region were held each month in locations around Inhotim. These events were selected by a team of curators whose members had close cultural ties to the city.

At the same time, numerous cooperations with other institutions around the world serve to present international as well as national art. A dedicated curatorial team in New York, for example, advises Inhotim on the acquisition of new works.

Inhotim also runs an extensive educational program for schoolchildren. Through innovative methodology, children are given a new way of approaching art and nature. They gain an awareness of different ways of life and living spaces and learn how these influence each other. This equips them with the knowledge for developing sustainable ways of living for the future. Inhotim also has its own orchestra dedicated to the training of young musicians.

Together with the related tourism infrastructure, such as restaurants and hotels, Inhotim is one of the most important economic contributors and employers in the region, offering young people in particular opportunities for the future.

Inhotim is not only a place for the interplay between art and nature; it is also a place that is open equally to people of all ages, educations, and backgrounds; a place that brings them together and inspires them.

← Yayoi Kusama, "Narcissus Garden Inhotim", 2009
Photo © Pedro Motta

→ Robert Irwin, "untitled", 2019
Photo © Brendon Campos

Studio–Agora–Site of Production

by Louisa Hutton and Matthias Sauerbruch

Museum of Contemporary Art Sydney
Rendering © Sauerbruch Hutton

To reflect upon a "utopia" for a museum district of the future, as the editors of this publication have asked us to do, is an interesting endeavor—both in the sense of "utopia" as a favored vision and with regard to the word's original meaning as an ideal place that serves as a projected alternative to the shortcomings of one's present existence.

In this light, the following text examines, amongst other examples, four case studies from our own practice in order to identify what we consider to be the key aspects of a successful museum district.

When we wrote about the "Museum as a Space of Encounter"[1] almost exactly twenty years ago, we were considering a design of ours that had just won the competition for the Museum of Contemporary Art and the Centre for the Moving Image in Sydney, Australia (2001). In this design, we had proposed to carve off a considerable amount of space from Circular Quay, a waterfront promenade that is very popular with Sydneysiders and tourists alike. We wanted to create an interface between the street and the museum that would make people enter the venue almost accidentally—people who otherwise wouldn't naturally be inclined to visit an art institution. At the same time, the museum would establish a low-threshold, curated public space—easily visible and accessible to everybody—that would be virtually free of commercial pressures. The museum was to be located diagonally opposite the Sydney Opera House and create not just a spatial, but also an architectural contrast, in that we saw our building less as an icon and more as an "enabling space". A sequence of public rooms would rise from the quayside through the various floors of the structure to create a set of increasingly specific and intimate environments. The curious visitor would be lured from the arbitrariness of everyday street life to environments dominated more and more by the aura of the art on display. For us, the museum was to offer the opportunity for encounter, firstly between visitors amongst each other—tourists and locals alike—but also between visitors and the museum and the diverse artifacts of its varied programs. The artist Rémy Zaugg wrote approximately at that time that a museum of contemporary art ought to work like a surrogate of the artist's workshop; it ought to provide the kind of intimacy that comes with the meeting between the maker and the viewer of art in the unprotected space of production. In fact, the confrontation with a work in a museum not only provides a proxy meeting with a particular artist, but also offers (in the acts of understanding and interpreting) a reflection of aspects of one's own personality. It is obvious that such highly personal and sensitive encounters can only ever take place in a gallery space that offers the necessary degree of intimacy. Therefore, our proposal was to create a transition of spaces whose characteristics would span from the randomness of the city to the concentration of the studio, and in this would help to introduce a range for encounters with a broad variety of art.

The Museum Brandhorst (2002–2009) pretty much fulfills the proposed requirement for galleries, namely, to let art fill the various spaces and allow its presence to unfold in the best possible conditions. However, in this case the threshold space between street and gallery had to be compressed into a relatively compact foyer. This limitation in turn has led to repeated, more or less spontaneous takeovers of the spaces around the building by activities of the museum—beginning with its own opening party, which was celebrated in a large tent in the middle of the adjacent lawn. The Museum Brandhorst is part of the Munich Kunstareal, which includes some of Europe's most important collections. In between the various art institutions, this quarter offers some large open lawns that—in both atmosphere and use—are determined by the aura not just of the museums, but also of various higher education buildings located in the immediate neighborhood. As a consequence, these lawns have taken on the informal feel of a university campus and are used by students, neighbors, and visitors alike to rest, read, gather, play, picnic, and just lie about in the sun. There is a quiescent space in the Brandhorst building that—at the end of the museum tour—offers a lounge with a generous view across one of these lawns outside. Thus the view through a large corner window lets some of the outdoor atmosphere pass into the contemplative aura of the works by Cy Twombly one has seen—just as the museum ventures outside to use the public space for performances or extended exhibitions.

The Türkentor (2005–2010) is perhaps a good example of how art can integrate and affect the public realm within the city. Inhabiting a repaired gatehouse that had been preserved as a last remnant of the nineteenth-century barracks that had formerly occupied this site, "Large Red Sphere", a monumental work by Walter de Maria, not only dominates this former threshold space, but also radiates into the surrounding area. A highly polished, red granite ball 2.6 m in diameter weighs heavily on a single point on a plinth, stable, yet seemingly about to roll off. Its massiveness heightens the viewer's awareness of light, time, and material in this relatively small space. The singular gesture of tentative permanence gains particular prominence in contrast to the scarred fabric of its housing. It introduces a reductive, quiet, and introverted element that suffuses the everyday informality of the surrounding "urban playground" with a certain absolute, almost transcendental presence.

The Munich Kunstareal—much like the MuseumsQuartier in Vienna and the

Museum of Contemporary Art Sydney
Renderings © Sauerbruch Hutton

Brandhorst Museum Munich
Photos ©Annette Kisling/Sauerbruch Hutton

M9 Museum District in Mestre—was established on the terrain of a former military area. In other locations, various industrial sites have been turned into museum districts or exhibition galleries (Tate Modern, Zeche Zollverein) in a similar way. These adaptations illustrate the "structural change" of the European city that took place in the second half of the twentieth century, triggered by the economic shift from industry 2.0 to industries 3.0 and 4.0—that is, from mechanical to electronic and from local to globally networked production, more and more of it automated and increasingly digitally controlled. In parallel with this transformation, Western industrial countries witnessed a dynamic emergence of the service sector within which creative industries have gained greater prominence and economic importance. Cultural production has developed into a burgeoning market and has become an asset in the competition between cities—both as an attractor for the tourist industry, as well as a soft factor in the competition for human resources.

In 2013, Matthias co-curated the exhibition "Kultur:Stadt" (Culture:City) at the Akademie der Künste in Berlin[2] that reflected upon what is widely known as the "Bilbao effect". This Basque city not only accompanied its transformation from a center of the steel industry to a hub in global service networks with a significant renewal of its urban amenities such as parks and public transport infrastructure, but also put itself on the map with a spectacular iconic building: the Guggenheim Museum by Frank O. Gehry. This structure followed the path that had been beaten by the Opera House in Sydney and quickly became the best-known example for the powerful impact a piece of architecture can have on the soul and self-esteem of an entire community. The building helped to immediately turn Bilbao into a brand that expedited societal change. However, the emerging equation of "spectacular architecture + contemporary art = successful structural change" didn't add up in every case that followed. In some instances, the iconic structures that pursued the

Bilbao model became monumental follies of provincial hubris that have unfortunately remained uprooted and alien to their communities.

Successful as it may have been as an icon of change, the Gehry building itself did not really serve as a good example for a contemporary cultural building or quarter. On closer inspection, the Guggenheim Foundation turned out to be a typical example of an organization that sets the tone for the art that it presents. Just like the building it inhabits, it set out to curate spectacular shows largely intent on creating maximum attention and firing the global art market. Thus, in this museum, overwhelming affect replaces the potential of the careful encounter, while the aggressive creation of value tends to drown out more unexpected aspects of artistic exploration.

Economic renewal and neoliberal cultural politics apart, the Akademie der Künste exhibition in Berlin identified an agenda for the changed role played by cultural buildings and cultural programs in the context of the general loss of the public realm. With the transfer of much social interaction into digital networks and the ubiquitous commodification particularly of historic city centers, the European City seems to have lost its role as a place of meaningful political, social, and spiritual exchange. Where are the locations where citizens can interact without interference by media? What is the content that can catalyze a lasting sense of community, from where do new ideas emerge, and where can cherished values survive? No doubt museums and other cultural buildings such as the new libraries can have a role in this and can form agoras of kinds. They can act as islands of intellectual sanity in a sea of commercialism, as reservations of sense and sensuality in a world that is submerged by virtual simulacra of physical experience. In this they are more than a soft asset for a new economy starting up: they become a central focus of urban self-awareness, part of the spiritual glue that keeps the community together and alive.

The M9 Museum District in Mestre (2010–2019) serves as an interesting study on the survival of a community's culture. Located on the "terra ferma", it can be seen as the reverse mirror image of the island of Venice, which has become the epitome of the excessive impact of global tourism on a site of historical interest. Only 50,000 local inhabitants share the island city with 30 million annual visitors (counted prior to the coronavirus pandemic, that is), while 250,000 locals live on the mainland where very few visitors ever stray. For a number of reasons, the "real" Venetians have, over recent decades, been almost completely displaced from the island and now live in Mestre, from where they commute every morning to sheer up the tourist trade of "La Serenissima". The new M9 Museum District, however, did not necessarily set out to reverse this balance of forces. In fact, it is likely that it will be predominantly frequented by "Mestrini" rather than foreign visitors—but as opposed to the highly commercialized island, it could actually offer an opportunity for the production of local, contemporary culture that is uninhibited by the predominance of past glories and their commodification.

The site of the new M9 museum district used to be occupied by a convent that had been secularized in Napoleonic times. It subsequently was used by the military for over a century and thus had been totally inaccessible to the public. Merely opening this area up for the new district has already had a positive effect on Mestre. We established a new piazzetta in its center, connecting it to the fine network of streets and alleyways that characterize the historic cities in the Veneto. Since this opening, the flow of pedestrian and bicycle traffic crisscrosses the area, and a restaurant and café invite passersby to rest. The actual museum building is equally hospitable on the ground floor with its offer of a multifunctional auditorium as well as a small media library, shop, and restaurant for immediate access. On two upper floors, a new museum of the twentieth century has been established that is the first totally digital museum of its kind (certainly in Italy). On the top floor there is a 900 m^2 sized, column-free, top-lit gallery that offers museum conditions of international standards for changing exhibitions. In addition, there are several places for didactic activities as well as facilities for administration, workshops, delivery, and storage.

In the other buildings of the district, the ground floors are occupied with spaces for commercial activity and public exchange: an art gallery, a bookshop, and a store for sporting articles as well as the representation of the local football club have established themselves. In the dormitory building of the former convent/barracks, co-working spaces are on offer for fledgling businesses. The former cloister/courtyard of the convent is now covered by a large freestanding umbrella roof, so that this protected outdoor space has also become a popular location for numerous open-air celebrations, presentations, and performances.

Similar to the Sydney scenario, the district offers a set of public rooms and a sequence of increasingly controlled spaces for the presentation of exhibitions, which in this instance are connected with a grand staircase that continues the logic of Mestre's alleyways into the building and right up to the top floor. Similarly to the Munich Kunstareal, the former military enclosure has been opened up and the terrain seamlessly woven into the fabric of the surrounding city. The entire district offers an aura of relaxed urbanity of a very Italian kind. Mestre's potential, however, surely lies in the simultaneity of excellent facilities with a somewhat remote location; it could become an ideal place of unprecedented production both in terms of art, museology, and a new kind of city life.

The museum had been open for just one year before the pandemic shut down all cultural life in Europe, and has since been in hibernation. However, the urban space with its various offerings was adopted by the local population almost from day one, partially simply because the new routes offer convenient shortcuts as well as informal places to gather. Whether the district will meet its anticipated potential as a crucial nexus in the community is still uncertain and will surely be a question of good programming and management. Unfortunately, the artistic directorship has already changed twice since the building works were finished, and another beginning is imminent.

Brandhorst Museum
Munich
Photo © Annette Kisling/
Cy Twombly Foundation

As a matter of fact, the exhibition program in the gallery on the third floor will start up with a retrospective of our own work in September 2021. Due to the exceptional circumstances, this will actually be the first exhibition that has been specifically produced for this space, as all shows held there hitherto were ready-mades from other institutions. So in a way this exhibition represents the inauguration of the space as a site of production. Obviously, we were pleased and honored by the invitation to show our work, in particular as this exhibition will provide us with the unique opportunity to combine the "real thing" with the products of representation (models, drawings, photographs, films) that are usual for architecture exhibitions.

Furthermore, to some degree we see this installation as a continuation of our urban work beyond the usual limitations of the architectural contract. One could describe it as an act of cultural activism; a first contemporary intervention of culture of the kind one would wish the district to host frequently from now on.

The exhibition will be mostly a physical project that follows a long absence of such presentations due to the various lockdowns. For more than a year, the museums across Europe—and elsewhere in the world—have been closed or accessible only in a very limited way. This has been a very frustrating experience, but it has also been—by default—an excellent testing ground for the virtual production and dissemination of culture. Everything we were doing in the last year had to be done via the Internet. Work happened day-in, day-out on Zoom or similar platforms from morning to evening; and after work, over the weekends, the routine carried on: culture on one's laptop, such as the Berlin Philharmonic Orchestra in livestream, films of old productions by the Schaubühne, a curated tour through the exhibition at various galleries, an interactive visit to the Louvre, the Met, the Rijksmuseum (you name it), or increasingly the Arte Mediathek, MUBI, and, ultimately, Netflix. In this context, architecture happened on Instagram or through recorded lectures, symposia, blogs, and films.

M9 Museum District
Venice Mestre
Photo © Jan Bitter

How we all miss the real experience!!

If the Internet had ever been viewed as a utopia for culture, 2020 certainly provided the hardest possible landing. The Internet is of course wonderful regarding accessibility; you can find out about almost anything in a very short time and with little effort, and your message can reach thousands of people instantaneously. If you have important content to disseminate, your reach will be without limit—except you have to compete with thousands of other users who think just the same.

To be a good painter, you have to train your skills; to be a sculptor or sculptress, you have to master your material; to be an architect, your construction has to resist decay and entropy. As a theater person, you have to strike a chord with your ensemble, and as a film director, you have to manage a huge crew. Every cultural production happens with the resistance of some sort of "material", and quite often you sense and appreciate the struggle of opposing forces that (if successful) lead to common, synergetic results. The Internet as a medium offers some technical limitations, but of course little resistance as such, and hence—culturally speaking—it is best when it communicates something that has already been produced elsewhere. Even then, the "cultural experience" is limited. One has to rely on one's previous "live" experiences to be able to simulate the reality of one of those performances or visits, and as memory starts to fade, the virtual event becomes more and more lacking. Of course, you can try to make yourself at home in the world of 280-character messages and low-resolution mini videoclips, but it is like starting to write a book while voluntarily reducing your normal vocabulary to a fraction of its size.

For architecture, the predicament is even worse. The communication of the complexities of space has always been difficult, if not impossible, with the two-dimensional media of photography and film. Now the contextualization of the object of this communication has become totally unpredictable. While Walter Benjamin had been confused by the meaning of an image of a cathedral that finds itself on the living-room wall, the predicament of the artwork in the age of digital dissemination is far worse. On the Internet, the context of any cultural product is highly corrupted and completely random, as everything competes with everything for on-screen attention, and this competition is certainly not won by information that is complex or subtle. The Internet can never be a utopia, as its content consists of a simultaneity of everything and the possibility of its continuous and ubiquitous consumption clearly renders it the ultimate non-place.

In 2021—following a year of pandemic-enforced abstinence—we are longing for precision of place and specificity of content, and in this context "Kunstareale" and museum districts could indeed offer a kind of countermodel to our current lockdown reality. Real locations, real experiences, and real meetings have gained enormously in desirability during this "year of want", and "the analog" has quite clearly won a competition that it never knew it wanted to enter.

So finally, to sum up this particular stock-taking exercise, these are the key aspects that we believe to have learned from our work with museum districts:

→ Reflection on culture is important for everybody and should be made as accessible as possible. At the same time, encounters with art need protected spaces. The architecture of museums has to be both open and inviting, but also determined to serve the art on display.

→ Museum districts are amongst the few urban places that are still protected from the ubiquitous commercialism that has tainted the public realm. They can act as modern-day agoras. When rooted in their communities, they can be places of informal urbanity that are central to their cities' souls.

→ To keep cultural traditions alive and continuously strive to discover new contemporaneities, museum districts must also act as places of production. Shared work can provide content and identity, and the architectural locus serves as an anchor point for the exploration of both physical as well as digital techniques and technologies.

1 Matthias Sauerbruch/Louisa Hutton, "The Museum as a Space of Encounter", in: Sauerbruch Hutton Archive 1, Basel 2006, pp. 146–151.

2 Matthias Sauerbruch, "Culture:City—Content and Form", in: Wilfried Wang (ed.), "Culture:City" (exh. cat. Akademie der Künste, Berlin), Basel 2013, pp. 16–23.

LAC Lugano Arte e Cultura

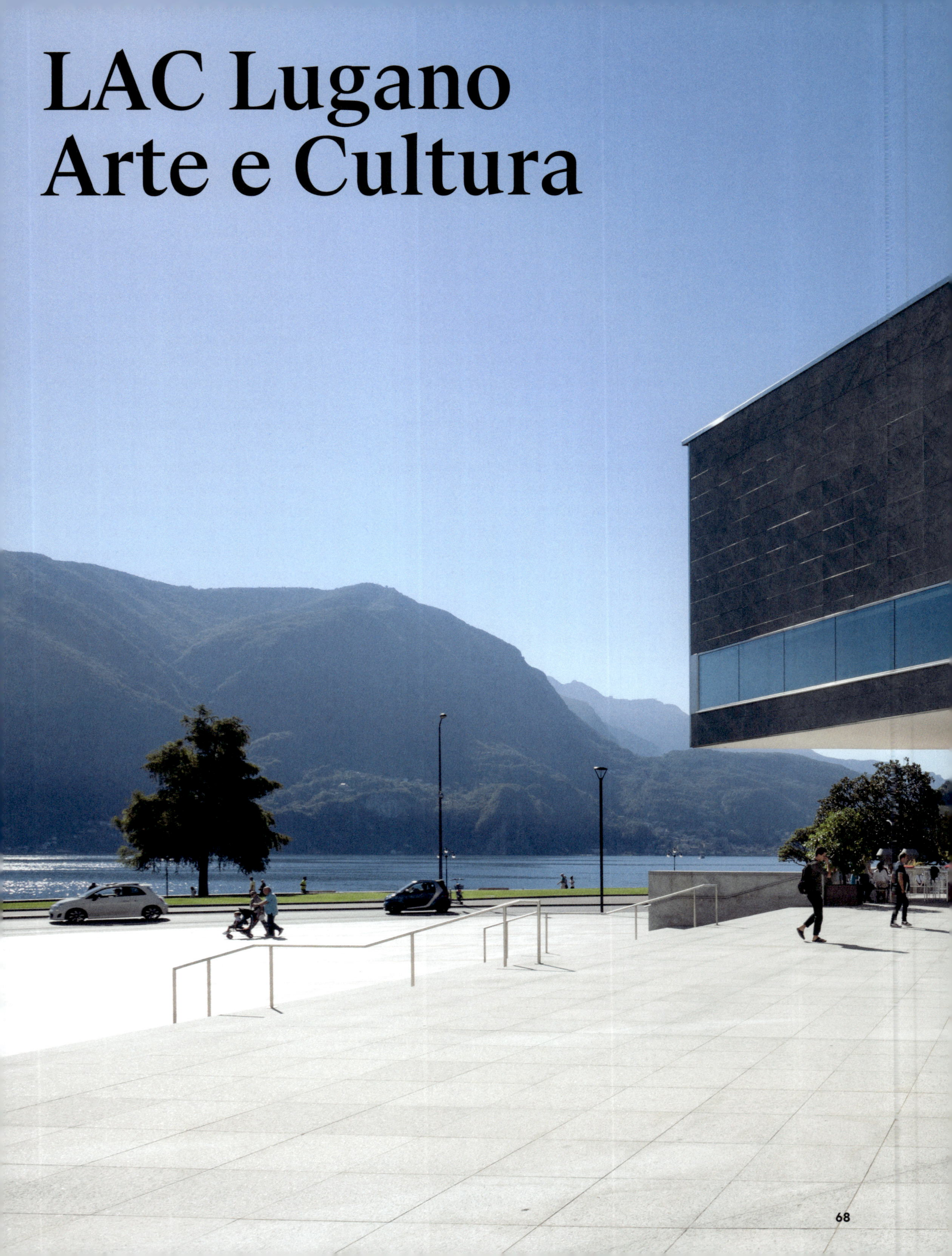

From Grand Hotel to a Cultural Spot

by Erwin Uhrmann

Lugano is characterized by its mild climate and spectacular scenic location. The LAC Lugano Arte e Cultura occupies what historically has been a key area on the shores of Lake Lugano. As the new cultural center of both the city and the Canton of Ticino, it acts as a cultural bridge to north and south, east and west for multilingual Switzerland. The center's program offers a broad spectrum of different art forms, from the visual arts to theater, and from performance and dance to music and literature.

Location	Switzerland, Lugano, Piazza Bernardino Luini 6
Opened	2015
Total area	40,000 m²
Number of cultural institutions	6
Leisure facilities & activities	cafés/restaurants, bookshop, park
Visitors/year	250,000
Architecture	Ivano Gianola
Website	www.luganolac.ch

History

The LAC Lugano Arte e Cultura may be a young cultural center, but it is able to look back upon a long pre-history. At the end of the fifteenth century, the Order of Friars Minor founded a convent and built the Church of Santa Maria degli Angioli at the southern entrance to the city; a hundred years later, the monastery was taken over by the Reformed Franciscans. In the nineteenth century, Lugano underwent what would prove to be the most decisive change in its history. The idea of converting the lakeside convent into a hotel had arisen in the first half of the century. In 1850, the brothers Giacomo and Filippo Ciani acquired the building and converted it into a hotel, opening it five years later as the Hotel du Parc; this launched the era of international tourism in Lugano. The fjord-like lake surrounded by mountains and the region's Mediterranean climate attracted illustrious visitors from all over Europe. Southern Switzerland had suddenly become easily accessible with the expansion of the railway, especially the construction in 1882 of the Gotthard tunnel, which provided a fast north-south connection through the Alps. The city authorities beautified the lakeshore and installed public lighting, giving the area a sophisticated flair.

↑ Aerial view of the LAC Lugano Arte e Cultura
Photo © 2015 LAC

↖ Previous double page: LAC Lugano Arte e Cultura
Photo © 2015 LAC/Studio Pagi

The Hotel du Parc—which at the time of its founding was the only hotel between Milan and Lucerne—hosted a number of well-known aristocratic and intellectual personalities, such as Empress Elisabeth of Austria-Hungary, French Empress Eugénie, Thomas Cook, and John Ruskin. Although the hotel was expanded with additions and extensions, other hotel operations rapidly became established in the immediate vicinity. The newer luxury inns soon rivalled the du Parc, which at the turn of the century was renamed Grand Hotel Palace and extended to five stories. This plunged the artistically and historically significant Church of Santa Maria degli Angioli, which was directly adjacent to the hotel, into deep shadow, causing it serious damage and resulting in a decades-long legal dispute between the new hotel owner and the Canton of Ticino. The church, which houses the most important Renaissance artwork in Switzerland—the large fresco "The Passion and Crucifixion of Christ" by Da Vinci's pupil Bernardino Luini—, had to undergo extensive restoration. The piazza in front of the LAC is named after Luini.

Aerial view of the LAC
Lugano Arte e Cultura
Photo © 2015 LAC

The once famous hotel experienced a gradual decline over the first half of the twentieth century and was shut down in 1965. It was auctioned off in 1980, subsequently changing hands several times. The building was destroyed by fire in 1993, except for its two main façades.

The City of Lugano then acquired the ruins of the former Grand Hotel with the plan to revitalize it and convert it into a casino. This idea was abandoned in favor of a new urban planning concept that aimed to transform the former hotel into a cultural complex that would be the new cultural center of Lugano. The city announced an architectural competition for the development of the project, receiving submissions from 122 international architectural firms. Fifteen entries advanced to the second round and four to the third. In 2002, the Swiss architect Ivano Gianola was announced the winner.

In 2004, Lugano City Council gave the project the green light; preparatory work began two years later, and in 2010 construction commenced. The costs of the new construction were publicly financed, with the restoration of the structural elements of the former hotel and monastery funded privately. After five years of construction, the LAC Lugano Arte e Cultura opened on September 12, 2015.

The center's program covers a wide spectrum of art forms ranging from music, performance, contemporary dance, opera, and ballet to the visual arts, literature, and theater. It also runs educational and outreach programs as well as discussion forums.

The Museo d'arte della Svizzera (MASI Lugano) was created through the merger of the Museo Cantonale d'Arte and the Museo d'Arte Lugano and housed in the three-story museum wing. It has had a second location in the Palazzo Reali since 2019.

To mark the site's fifth anniversary, some areas were structurally adapted and developed further; the foyer, for example, now houses a site-specific work by artist Christine Streuli.

Architecture

The site consists of newly built structures, revitalized buildings and spaces, and outdoor areas such as the piazza and park. The old section was originally a convent that had been converted into a grand hotel in the mid-nineteenth century by the architect Chierichetti (1798–1875). Chierichetti preserved a large part of the monastery's structure, creating an L-shaped building with two massive neoclassical façades, one facing the lake and the other the park. Chierichetti added a third floor to the building's lakeside section; later, due to the increase in tourism, the hotel was extended to five stories on all sides. The Church of Santa Maria degli Angioli and parts of the original monastery still remain.

When the decision was taken in 2000 to redevelop the area, the revitalization of the hotel ruins was made a requirement of the architecture competition. The winner of the three-stage competition, the Swiss architect Ivano Gianola, is an exponent of the Ticino school of architecture known as Tendenza; the LAC Lugano Arte e Cultura is considered to be his most important design. In the central new building he created a large entrance hall, which links the park at the rear with the Piazza Bernardino Luini and opens up a view of the lake. The entrance hall houses the reception area, ticket office, bookshop, and restaurant.

LAC Lugano Arte e Cultura

← The façade of the LAC Lugano Arte e Cultura

→ Piazza Bernardino Luini seen from the event rooms on the third floor of the LAC Lugano Arte e Cultura

↓ The theater and concert hall

Photos © 2015 LAC

↘ The orchestral pit of the LAC can accommodate up to 60/70 musicians
Photo © D. Vass

The 1,000-seat theater and concert hall has been designed as a modular and multifunctional versatile space that can be used for dance, performance, and many other art forms. A studio stage and multi-functional room—which also offers a view of the surroundings and lake—offer further possibilities for performative events. Outside there is an open-air amphitheater.

The load-bearing structures of the new building are made of reinforced concrete and partly of steel. Green marble and red travertine were used for the exterior façade; the doors are made of stainless steel and the interior floors are made from Ticino granite. The interior of the theater and concert hall is lined with the reddish wood of the hazel pine. The entire area's construction has produced a particularly quiet location that emits barely any sound or vibration.

The three-floor, 2,500 m² museum wing was built to house the Museo d'arte della Svizzera italiana (MASI Lugano). At the visually striking, pointed edge of the museum building is a panoramic window that provides a spectacular view of the lake and surrounding landscape. The piazza in front, lined with Ticino granite, is laid out as a modern agora—a reference to ancient places of celebration and assembly—and functions as a link between the architecture, landscape, and the city.

Structure

LAC Lugano Arte e Cultura covers a total area of 40,000 m² in the south of the city on the Riva Caccia, directly on Lake Lugano. Bordered on its west and east sides by the lake and park, the site connects the old town in the north with newer districts in the south. It comprises a large entrance hall, a multifunctional theater and concert hall, a studio theater, an event room, and atelier; there is also a bookshop, a bistro, a café, and restaurant. At the front, towards the lake, is the 2,500 m² Piazza Bernadino Luini; to the rear is the 5,000 m² park. These two public areas are accessible around the clock; the institutions have fixed opening hours. The area can be reached from the center of Lugano by bus using public transport, or on foot.

← The panoramic window of the museum with the work of the Swiss artist Not Vital
Photo © 2019 MASI Lugano

↙ View of the exhibition "Orizzonte Nord-Sud" at the MASI Lugano
Photo © 2015 LAC

↘ A concert by the Orchestra della Svizzera italiana in Piazza Luini
Photo © Cdt/Gabriele Putzu 2020

→ The Agora with its park hosts the summer festival "LAC en plein air"
Photo © 2019 LAC

Organization

The cultural center is a non-profit organization. The directorship is responsible for the programming and operations. In addition to its own artistic season (theater, dance, and music), the LAC hosts a resident orchestra (Orchestra della Svizzera italiana) and a resident company (Compagnia Finzi Pasca), the MASI Lugano, an independent foundation responsible for art exhibitions, and LuganoMusica, responsible for classical music. Equipped with important public spaces such as an open-air theater, a hall, and a piazza, it is a public place in the city that is full of life all year long.

The center has a total annual budget of twenty-eight million Swiss francs, forty-six percent of which is provided by the city of Lugano. The remaining fifty-four percent of funding comes from sponsors, donations, entrance fees, and other income.

The center's construction costs, borne by the city of Lugano, amounted to 210 million Swiss francs. The restoration of the former hotel and monastery was privately financed with a further 100 million Swiss francs.

Programming

The LAC Lugano Arte e Cultura follows a multidisciplinary approach to elaborate its program. It has its own artistic directorship for the dance and theater season, while the classical music season is directed by the independent Foundation LuganoMusica; MASI Lugano Foundation, another independent foundation, is responsible for art exhibitions. In the public spaces, LAC runs an extensive program of music, theater, concerts, installations, and a summer season. The cultural center is active as a producer and co-producer with the aim of supporting and promoting local artists. The program is very international; LAC welcomes orchestras, dance companies, and artists from abroad.

The In Residence project offers orchestras, companies, and artists a longer-term platform for their artistic work. The current Orchestra in Residence is the Orchestra della Svizzera italiana, whose history as a radio orchestra is an international success story that dates back to 1935. The Company in Residence is the Compagnia Finzi Pasca. Founded in 2011 by Antonio Vergamini, Daniele Finzi Pasca, Hugo Gargiulo, Julie Hamelin Finzi and Maria Bonzanigo, the company blends dance, theater, acrobatics, circus, and opera. Both resident organizations exert substantial influence on the center's artistic program with their work.

← "Prismatica" transforms the Piazza Luini into a giant kaleidoscope
Photo © 2018 LAC/Studio Pagi

→ Behind the scenes of the "The Barber of Seville"
Photo © 2018 LAC

In the field of visual art, the MASI Lugano forms an artistic bridge between northern and southern Europe.

On display are contemporary art and works drawn from its extensive collection, which was amassed through the amalgamation of two separate museum collections. It contains works by Ticino artists and those who have worked in Italian-speaking Switzerland, as well as other Swiss and international artists. The museum also maintains an institutional partnership with the Collezione Giancarlo e Danna Olgiati, a remarkable collection of modern and contemporary art.

Impact

The LAC Lugano Arte e Cultura receives an average of 250,000 visitors per year. Since its opening it has become the home of several art and cultural institutions. Its architecture makes it a representative landmark in a spectacular landscape. In the span of only a few years, the MASI Lugano has surpassed most other Swiss museums in terms of visitor numbers, and so has affirmed itself as an important economic player in the tourism of the region. The LAC forms a cultural bridge to the regions south of the Alps, and is a place where different mindsets and currents from northern and southern Europe converge.

Planned on the threshold of the twenty-first century, the factors of ecology and sustainability have been essential to the LAC's orientation. The LAC was conceived as a social focal point in the spirit of sustainable urban planning. The newly created piazza is the largest public square in Lugano, located at the interface between the historic old town and the newer residential areas. The Belvedere Gardens-style park provides a place of recreation for the city's residents and links the residential areas to its rear with the cultural quarter.

Historically, the area has been a source of inspiration since the sixteenth century and reflects some of the most important cultural, infrastructural, and economic developments in Lugano and the Canton of Ticino: first as a monastery at the southern entrance to the city, then in the nineteenth century as the region's first hotel, which attracted international visitors and laid the foundation for Lugano's transformation into a sophisticated city of tourism. In the twenty-first century, the area—in a new, contemporary guise—became the key project for a development aimed at redefining the city in economic and social terms, expanding its international artistic network and increasing its global cultural footprint.

Performance of the students of the Conservatorio della Svizzera italiana in the free concerts "Hall in musica"
Photo © 2015 LAC

M9

A Sustainable Cultural District as the Key to Urban Development

by Erwin Uhrmann

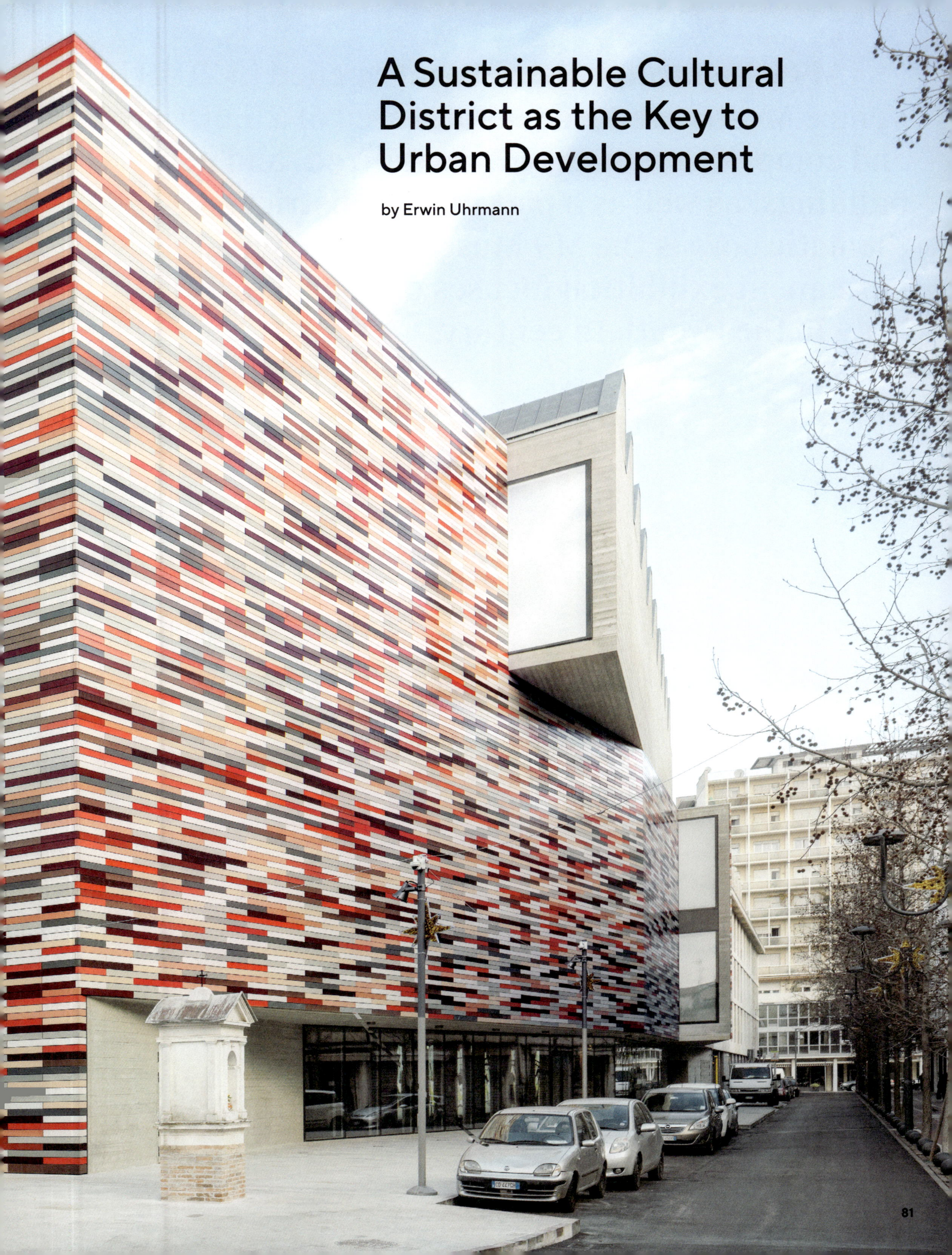

M9 is a cultural district that opened in 2018 in Venice Mestre. It covers a total area of 25,600 m² and comprises several old, revitalized, and new buildings, as well as a piazza. The district's thematic core is the M9 Museum, which in a permanent exhibition focuses on the history of Italy in the twentieth century.

Location	Italy, Mestre, Via Pascoli 11/city center
Opened	2018
Total area	25,600 m²
Number of cultural institutions	1
Leisure facilities & activities	cafés/restaurants
Visitors/year	60,000
Architecture	Sauerbruch Hutton (Louisa Hutton and Matthias Sauerbruch)
Website	www.m9museum.it

History and Architecture

According to legend, Mestre was founded by Mesthles, a companion of the Trojan hero Antenor. For centuries, Mestre formed the bridgehead to the great lagoon city of Venice, handling all traffic of passengers and goods. Its strategically important location often made Mestre the subject of territorial dispute between competing political players. For Venice, it acted as a bulwark to the mainland until Napoleon brought an end to the city-state's nearly 500-year-rule over Mestre in 1797. Following French and Austrian rule, Mestre became part of Italy in 1866 and was elevated to city status. From 1846 onwards, Mestre was connected to Venice via a railway bridge; a motorway bridge was added less than 100 years later. In 1926, Mestre and several other coastal towns were incorporated into Venice.

Mestre's development was severely affected by the construction of the Marghera port and industrial district at the beginning of the twentieth century, which brought the oil, metal, and shipbuilding industries to the area. The chemical industry in particular grew quickly following the Second World War, triggering a rapid growth in population. During this period, Mestre grew without any development plan in place. In the 1970s, rising oil prices pushed the industry into severe crisis. Jobs were lost on a massive scale and, just as quickly as Mestre had grown, it now became a "shrinking city". In the late 1990s, the massive petrochemical industry in Marghera came under severe criticism for the environmental damage caused by twenty years of dumping toxic waste into the lagoon. Venice's tourist boom also had an impact on Mestre. Industry was overtaken by the service sector, and by the start of the twenty-first century Mestre had become a "bedroom community" for locals and tourists. The city administration made numerous efforts to make Mestre more livable, for example by creating parks and redesigning the central Piazza Erminio Ferretto as a pedestrian zone. A citizens' committee was set up to discuss building a Mestre museum, which would provide an overview of local history from antiquity onward and exhibit archaeological finds.

↑ M9, aerial view
Photo © Alessandra Chemollo, courtesy M9 District

↖ Previous double page:
View of M9
Photo © Jan Bitter

This plan was ultimately abandoned, but in its place the "Mestre 900" project was implemented, which proposed the creation of a museum that would focus on the twentieth-century history of the region around Venice.

In 2005, the Fondazione di Venezia, a banking foundation of the former Cassa di Risparmio di Venezia, successively bought up a block of several old buildings opposite the Cathedral of San Lorenzo and next to the Piazza Erminio Ferretto. The foundation's objective was to improve the quality of life and create a new cultural district in Mestre. The district would serve as an urban and social reference point for the city's inhabitants and positively impact the community and future urban development. An international architecture competition was held, with several major architectural firms submitting their proposals on how to shape the district. The Berlin studio Sauerbruch Hutton emerged as the winner in 2010.

M9 became the key project in Mestre's reorientation in the 2010s. Open on all sides, it merges different parts of the city. The Fondazione di Venezia aimed to create both a place with which the local population could identify and a visitor attraction across from historic Venice. By 2013, Louisa Hutton and Matthias Sauerbruch had finalized their design for the museum, now with the abbreviated name M9, which was to focus on the history of Italy in the twentieth century.

Sauerbruch Hutton's previous projects had earned them a reputation as specialists in creating transition points between districts within urban structures. Their plan envisaged retaining part of the site's older structures—including a building from the 1970s and a former Benedictine monastery that had long been used as barracks—while also creating new buildings. The sixteenth-century monastery—the Convento Santa Maria delle Grazie—forms a kind of membrane between the old city, with its baroque and renaissance architecture, and modern Mestre, with its density of post-war residential buildings. This historically important building had long been inaccessible to the public. The architects

← Detail of the portico renovated by Sauerbruch Hutton

→ View of M9 covered courtyard of former convent
Photo © Jan Bitter

↗ View of M9

Photos © Alessandra Chemollo, courtesy M9 District

revitalized the old monastery, roofing over the inner courtyard and transforming it into a new urban gathering place that could also be used for concerts and festivals. The roof provides protection from the heat, especially in the hot summer months. To optimize visitor flow, Sauerbruch Hutton laid out the buildings along a diagonal approach leading from the monastery entrance through the inner courtyard and into the museum piazza. The four wings around the inner courtyard contain a children's library, co-working spaces, start-up companies, offices and shops. Behind the monastery is the museum piazza, which has quickly developed into a social gathering place. Two cavallerizze (horse stables) that had been located beside the piazza were demolished but then rebuilt in the same form using modern materials. One of these houses the Museum's technical rooms; the other houses a garden restaurant that is especially popular in the evenings.

M9—Museum of the 20th Century forms the heart of the site. Its façade and adjacent administration building are covered with tiles in seventeen different colors drawn from the Mestre cityscape and Venice that establish a visual connection with the Museum's surroundings. The gentle upward slant of the tiles is a reference to Italian Futurism. Three types of material dominate the Museum's interior: beechwood, which lines the ceilings; exposed concrete on the walls, which reflects the textures of various woods from the region; and trachyte, the stone used in the construction of Venice's houses, which lines the floor.

The glass walls on the ground floor and in the upper section of the auditorium, which slopes down to the basement floor, dissolve the boundaries between interior and exterior, inviting visitors and residents inside. While the Museum has a historical and socio-political focus, the Marina Bastianello Gallery on the ground floor of the administration building is devoted to both Italian and international contemporary art.

The cultural district was opened in 2018 and attracted 60,000 visitors in 2019.

Structure

Located in the center of Mestre, the M9 museum quarter is bordered to the south by Via Giosuè Carducci, to the west by Via Rosa, to the east by Via Brenta Vecchia, and to the north by Via Alessandro Poerio, which connects it to the central Piazza Erminio Ferretto. Via Cappuccina leads directly from the rail station to the quarter. Admission to the site is free, but tickets must be purchased for the Museum. In addition to the cafés and restaurants in the Museum, the museum piazza, and the former monastery, there are a number of other catering establishments nearby. The former monastery contains shops and office space for start-up businesses, and the covered inner courtyard is used for events.

In addition to its exhibition rooms, the M9 Museum houses an auditorium, shop, and café. Next to the Museum is an administration building used by museum staff.

↑ View of museum piazza

← View of M9, museum and administration building

→ M9—Museum of the 20th Century, inner view, third floor staircase

Photos © Jan Bitter

Organization

The M9 District and Museum are owned by the Fondazione di Venezia and managed by one directorate. The M9 Museum is responsible for all curatorial matters, while several committees, including a scientific board, are responsible for content. The Fondazione di Venezia provided the funds to cover the 110 million Euro construction budget. Operating costs are financed partly from the foundation's assets, ticket sales, and income from the rental of spaces and facilities.

Programming

The M9 District represents the core project in Mestre's reorientation strategy, which brings culture and social interaction to the fore. At the center of its educational and outreach activities stands the M9 Museum, whose permanent exhibit on two floors focuses on the history of Italy in the twentieth century. The concept behind the exhibition relies on a multimedia narration strategy that employs a range of current technologies to create an immersive experience for visitors. Over two floors, the exhibition presents a comprehensive survey of social and political events, as well as of the everyday world, over the course of time. The tour, which takes visitors through the themes and times of the twentieth century, is divided into eight zones, each with an encompassing social theme, starting with "The way we were and are". The topics range from demography, gender, family, state and law, economy, science, nutrition, progress, ecology, migration, education, and culture to lifestyle. Visitors can interact with the historic events shown, research and consume content at multimedia stations, trace developments, create models, and make connections. In this respect, M9 is not a traditional museum: "Its true protagonists are documents and materials serving visitors as a means to clearly follow a narration of the history of a century as it occurred in a specific area".[1] With this in mind, archive materials, films, photographs, texts, and documents of the twentieth century have been rendered accessible and interactive using new technologies. There are also temporary exhibitions covering architectural topics and a separate multimedia experience area for children, schools, and families. This area offers multimedia exhibitions for children as well as workshops and educational opportunities for teachers and families using innovative tools for learning.

Impact

The M9 District is the key project in Mestre's urban regeneration efforts. The approach is based on the Bilbao effect: Europe offers many successful examples of large cultural institutions and museums that have made key contributions to the growth and regeneration of urban areas.

The creation of the M9 District followed several visions for sustainable urban development. Ecological energy production, for example, played a central role. The new museum buildings were designed to incorporate a substantial number of active and passive steps that reduce energy requirements, CO_2 production, and the buildings' ecological footprint while employing natural and renewable resources and eco-friendly raw materials and construction methods. These steps include, in particular, the compact design of the main building and its intelligent mix of closed and glazed surfaces; the innovative application of mass activation; the careful choice of façade materials and envelope design solutions; extensive recourse to geothermal science; and additional energy production from photovoltaic panels on the roof. The priority given to accommodating start-ups and companies in the field of the life sciences in the monastery underlines this aspect of sustainable development. Owing to the encouraging response to and positive developments set in motion by the quarter, additional buildings around the M9 District are now to be revitalized and integrated into the new urban concept. Like many other cultural quarters, the M9 District continues to grow. Conceived from the start as an integral and unifying district, the area provides the stimulus for a sustainable and social urban development that aims to return public space to the people and create an environment for positive social development through cultural education and communication.

1 Cesare de Michelis, "M9 and the urban regeneration of Mestre", in: "M9, Museum of the 20th Century", Venice 2018, p. 36.

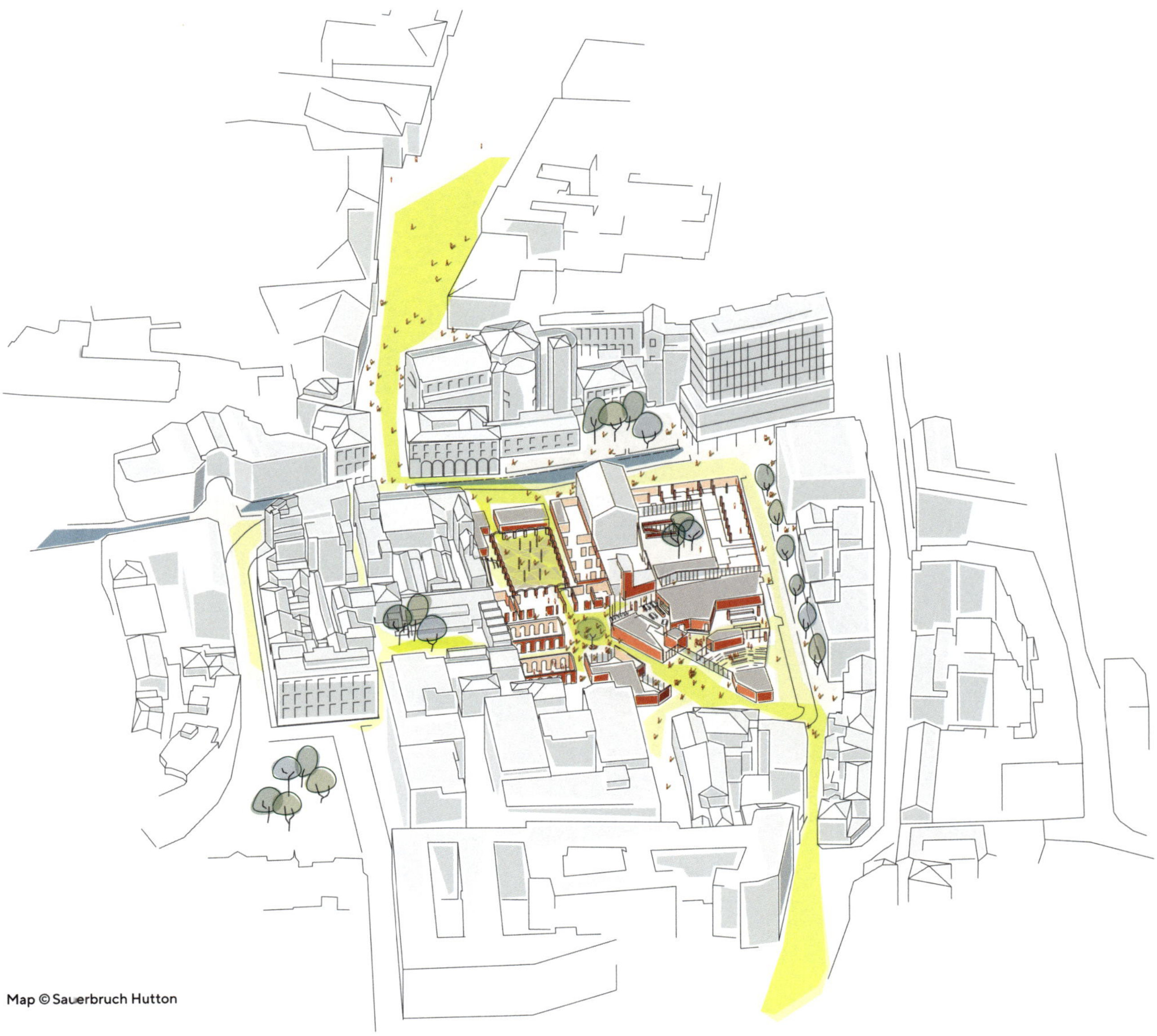

Map © Sauerbruch Hutton

MASS MoCA Massachusetts Museum of Contemporary Art

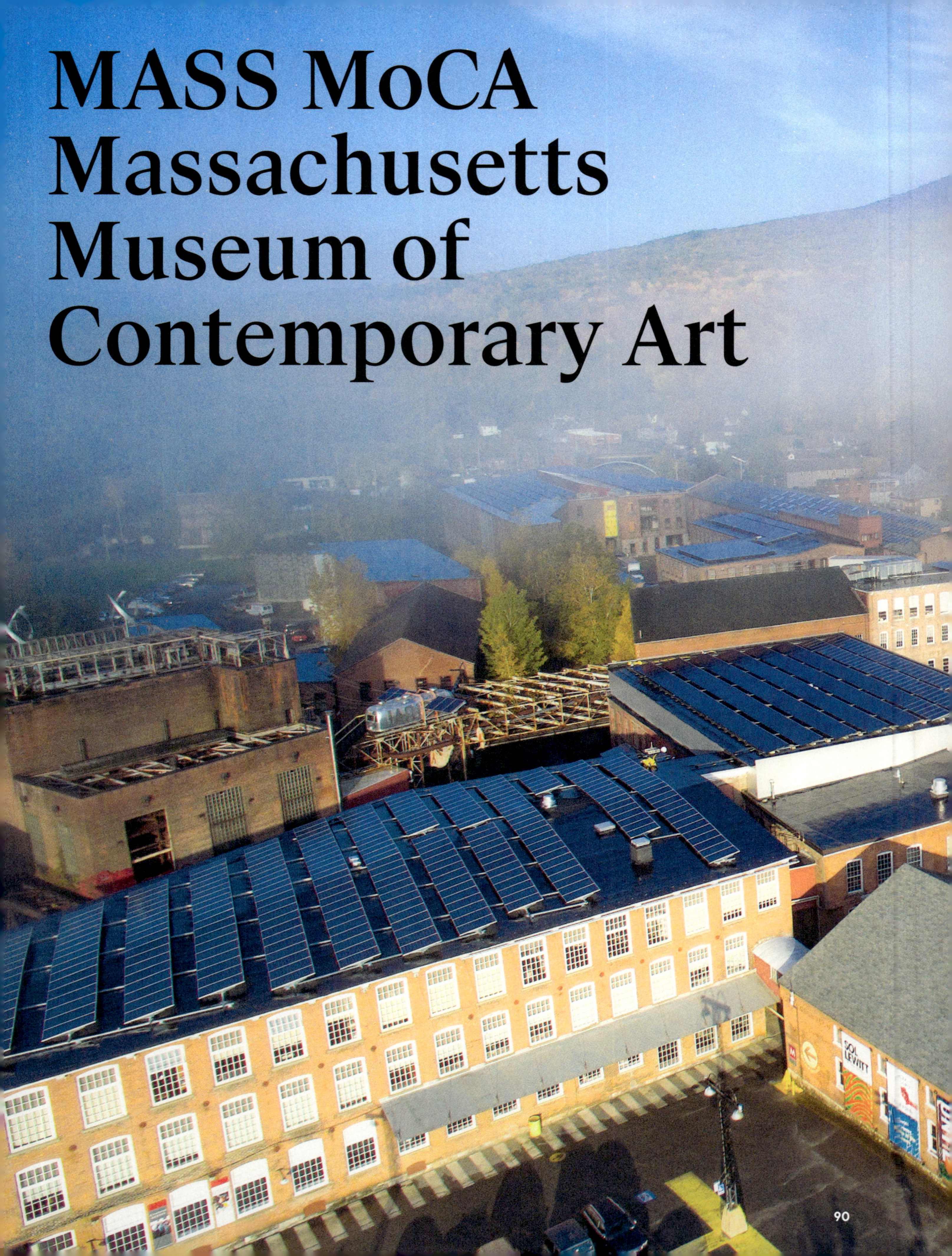

New Art in Old Halls

by Irene Preißler

Developed on a former industrial site, today MASS MoCA is one of the most extensive cultural centers in the United States, with around 23,000 m² (250,000 square feet) of exhibition space and 10,200 m² (110,000 square feet) dedicated to performances on its 64,000 m² (690,000 square feet), twenty-six-building site. All forms of art are present: from sculpture, painting, installation, photography, music, dance, film, and theater to cross-genre collaborations. What sets MASS MoCA apart is the fact that a large number of works are created or workshopped directly on site, and with a studio residency program, there are dozens of artists living and working at MASS MoCA throughout the entire year.

Location	USA, Massachusetts, North Adams, 1040 MASS MoCA Way/downtown
Opened	1999
Total area	approx. 64,000 m² (690,000 square feet)
Number of cultural institutions	26 buildings with exhibition and performance spaces, galleries, cultural facilities, and offices
Leisure facilities & activities	public open spaces, shops, cafés/restaurants
Visitors/year	250,000
Architecture	Bruner/Cott & Associates
Website	www.massmoca.org

History

From the late eighteenth to the mid-nineteenth century, the area was home to various small industrial businesses such as shoe manufacturers, joineries, milliners, brickwork machining shops, a sawmill, marble works, wagon and sleigh makers, and an ironworks.

In 1860, the printers O. Arnold and Company, a manufacturer specializing in fabric printing, settled in the area. Through government and military contracts, Arnold Print Works grew into one of the largest and most important employers in North Adams. By the end of the 1890s, twenty-five of the twenty-six buildings still standing as part of the MASS MoCA complex today were already in existence. Arnold Print Works had become one of the world's leading companies in the printing sector, with around 3,200 employees. Nonetheless, in 1942, following the Great Depression, falling textile prices forced the company to close their facilities at the site and relocate to smaller premises in the neighboring town of Adams.

The site was acquired that same year by the Sprague Electric Company. Equipped with state-of-the-art technology, the company manufactured weapon components during the Second World War on behalf of the government, including parts for the atomic bomb. Following the War, Sprague Electric developed into a renowned research and development center with 4,137 employees, supplying products to the booming electronics industry, as well as to projects such as the Gemini moon missions. In 1981, Sprague Electric was sold to the Penn Central Corporation and in 1985 renamed American Annuity Group. Declining sales and ever-stronger pricing pressure, however, led to the facility's closure the same year.

↖ Previous double page:
Aerial view of MASS MoCA campus
Photo © Douglas Mason, courtesy of MASS MoCA

↓ Aerial view of the MASS MoCA campus and neighboring streets
Photo: Larry Smallwood, courtesy of MASS MoCA

It was only one year after its closure, in 1986, that Thomas Krens, then director of the Williams College Museum of Art, first considered using the former factory grounds for cultural purposes and displaying large works of contemporary art that could not be shown in conventional museums or galleries. With the approval of the mayor and the local government, the decision was made to transform the site into an art district.

In 1988, financial and political setbacks threatened the project's realization. Thomas Krens left the area to become director of the Solomon R. Guggenheim Museum in New York. Joseph C. Thompson, the museum's founding director, lobbied tirelessly for the project's continuation. Thanks to the broad support of the public, the city, and the support of private donors, planning was finally able to continue. In 1996, Massachusetts Governor William Weld released $18 million in state grant funds first appropriated under Governor Michael Dukakis's term, matching $8 million raised by project supporters.

The first exhibitions on the campus were held in 1996, with a 1,000 m^2 (10,800 square feet) multimedia installation by David Byrne. MASS MoCA officially opened its doors in 1999 and has since become one of the largest centers for contemporary visual and performing arts in the United States.

← MASS MoCA Courtyard, with Natalie Jeremijenko's "Tree Logic", 1999
Photo: Zoran Orlić, courtesy of MASS MoCA

→ Franz West: "Les Pommes d'Adam", 2007, Hall Art Foundation at MASS MoCA, Installation view with the Boiler House in background
Photo: Joseph Thompson, courtesy of MASS MoCA

Further conversion work took place over the following years. Building 7 was adapted in 2006 for a retrospective of wall drawings by conceptual artist Sol Le Witt, a cooperation with the Yale University Art Gallery and Williams College. Joe's Field was added in 2010, and the first Solid Sound Festival in collaboration with the indie rock band Wilco took place the same year. The third phase of conversion work was completed in 2017 with the opening of Building 6, housing major installations by Laurie Anderson, Louise Bourgeois, Jenny Holzer, and James Turrell.

The history of MASS MoCA, then, is a microcosm of a former factory site's two hundred years of economic, industrial, and architectural changes, spanning the arc from industrialization to post-industrialization.

Architecture

Bridges, courtyards, endless expanses of windows, and red brick façades give the complex's architecture its unique appearance.

"Ringed by mountains and crossed by the north and south branches of the Hoosic River, the site was a village unto itself, oddly medieval in its dense urban massing. Beyond the quantity of stunning spaces, their variety made the mill uniquely suited to contemporary art's requirements", [1] said Joseph Thompson, MASS MoCA's founding director.

The original masterplan for transforming the former industrial complex into a cultural district was developed by the architect Simeon Bruner (Bruner/Cott & Associates), along with Frank Gehry, Robert Venturi, and David Childs of Skidmore, Owings & Merrill. The final design was by Bruner/Cott and Associates of Boston, who remained the project's chief architect through 2021.

In total, the site comprises twenty-six buildings, which were converted and renovated in phases.

Phase One mostly involved demolition work, while the basic structure and features of the historic buildings—such as the interlocking courtyards, bridges, walkways, columns, exposed pipes and the unique red brickwork—were consciously preserved. Consequently, a few of the buildings have retained their original low ceilings, while others have had these removed in order to double or even triple the ceiling height to accommodate large art installations. Building 5, for example, has the dimensions of a football field, with a length of 100 m and a height of nearly 10 m.

In Phase Two, Building 7 was restored and adapted to display works by the conceptual artist Sol Le Witt. A three-story skylighted staircase was built between Buildings 7 and 5. In 2013, a concrete structure was specially renovated to house a selection of large-scale sculptures from The Hall Foundation's collection.

Building 6 was converted into gallery spaces in Phase Three, with an added glass ceiling creating a light-filled, double-height central passageway. Renovations and reconfigurations also created a two-story event space, a catering kitchen, restroom facilities, art storage, a loading dock, and a green room for festival events. Visitors can thus experience art in an extraordinary architectural site.

Organization

MASS MoCA is an independent not-for-profit institution with around 130 employees. They are managed by a director, who in turn reports to a board of trustees. The land and buildings are owned by the City of North Adams and leased to the private foundation. The site is financed through earned income as well as private donations and public and private grants. Funding is also generated by leasing space to independent and autonomous external businesses.

Structure

MASS MoCA was developed on a former industrial site in the city of North Adams, in the Berkshires of Western Massachusetts. It is located three hours north of New York by car and three hours west of Boston.

Surrounded by gentle hills, the site is bordered on one side by the Hoosic River—which also crosses through the grounds—and by Marshall Street on the other. The approx. 64,000 m^2 (690,000 square feet) complex comprises twenty-six buildings, four courtyards, outdoor art installations, green areas and the outdoor venue Joe's Field for festivals and concerts.

The main entrance courtyards, which accommodate shops and external businesses, are freely accessible to the public around the clock, as is the park at the corner of Main Street and MASS MoCA Way. All other areas are open only during museum opening hours. The Kidspace gallery, main entrance lobby, Hunter Theater lobby and mezzanine are also admission free.

MASS MoCA is not directly accessible by public transport. Trains run from New York to Albany, which is a little more than an hour's drive from North Adams, or from Boston to Pittsfield, roughly a half-hour drive away. Buses run from New York City and Boston to Pittsfield and Williamstown, which are approximately thirty minutes and ten minutes away by car.

→ Installation view of Liz Glynn: "The Archaeology of Another Possible Future", 2017
Courtesy of the artist and Paula Cooper Gallery, New York and Susanne Vielmetter Los Angeles Projects
Photo: Steven Probert, courtesy of MASS MoCA

North Adams, Massachusetts, United States of America

Programming

The visual arts at MASS MoCA focus especially on large-scale installations that would not be feasible in most museums due to their size. The program includes thematic group exhibitions, temporary solo exhibitions, and commissions by artists such as Nick Cave, Alex Da Corte, Ann Hamilton, Teresita Fernández, Katharina Grosse, Cai Guo-Qiang, Glenn Kaino, Cauleen Smith, Simon Starling, and many others, as well as long-term solo presentations of the works of Laurie Anderson, Louise Bourgeois, Jenny Holzer, Sol LeWitt, and James Turrell, who is represented with nine light installations in the galleries and a Skyspace situated in a former water tank on the campus grounds. Additionally, around seventy-five events and performances take place every year. These range from dance, cabaret, film, and live music to avant-garde theater and work-in-process productions.

MASS MoCA's visitors have the opportunity to experience the visual and performing arts in all their forms, as well as the chance to witness all phases of production and creation from beginning to completion. The range of genres includes sculpture, installation, painting, photography, dance, theater, film, music, and much more. This diversity creates exciting new opportunities for collaboration.

Kidspace is a child-centered gallery featuring exhibitions that address important social issues, along with a do-it-yourself artmaking studio and Art Bar—all free of charge.

Some spaces on MASS MoCA's campus are rented out to shops and galleries, such as ROAM, an African art and photo gallery, Ferrin Contemporary, which showcases ceramic art, Eckert Fine Art, which specializes in post-war and contemporary art, and The Artist Book Foundation.

Several residency programs offer artists the opportunity to live and work on site. These include fabrication residencies for the preparation of exhibitions, performing art residencies for the development of theater and dance productions, and The Studios at MASS MoCA, which offers studio residencies of two to eight weeks. The studios are located within the MASS MoCA complex. Artists are given free access to the museum and partner institutions. Here they can network with other artists and make use of common resources, such as the financial and business coaching offered by Assets for Artists.

As a complement to the galleries and exhibition spaces, numerous art installations, free for visitors to view, are on display in the outdoor areas. These include Martin Puryear's monumental sculpture "Big Bling"; the sound installation "Harmonic Bridge" by Bruce Odland and Sam Auinger, in which a drone in C major merges with the sounds of passers-by and traffic; Richard Nona's work "Cut Back Through (for Bjorn)", consisting of three armchairs and five stools made of granite; and the bulbous pink sculptures of Franz West's "Les Pommes d'Adam", which takes its name and inspiration from the male Adam's apple.

There are also open spaces where people can meet and relax, cafés, restaurants, and an on-site brewery. In the summer, a wide variety of events are held, from film screenings to music festivals such as the bi-annual Solid Sound festival. The summers also bustle with the presence of the Bang on a Can Summer Music Festival and Music Institute, a program for young composers and performers.

↖ James Turrell, "Perfectly Clear" (Ganzfeld), 1991
Gift of Jennifer Turrell
© James Turrell, photo: Florian Holzherr

← Installation view of Cauleen Smith: "We Already Have What We Need", 2019
Courtesy of the artist and Corbett vs. Dempsey, Chicago
Photo: David Dashiell, courtesy of MASS MoCA

→ Installation view of Katharina Grosse: "One Floor Up More Highly", 2010
Photo: Arthur Evans, courtesy of MASS MoCA

With its wide variety of cultural activities and programs, MASS MoCA strives to be a dynamic platform that encourages the exchange between creating art and experiencing it, and where everyone feels welcome: "We want you to feel at home here, whether it's your 100th visit to a contemporary art museum or your first."[2]

Impact

While MASS MoCA is first and foremost a center of creativity for visitors and artists, it has also contributed significantly to the city's economic upturn with its shops, restaurants, businesses, and as one of the largest employers in the region. Estimates by economists at nearby Williams College place MASS MoCA's annual contribution to the regional economy at $ 52 million yearly.

MASS MoCA's Assets for Artists program supports artists—who play a key role in producing an active society and flourishing economy—in achieving their financial and economic goals. The program is aimed specifically at local artists in order to support community-building initiatives, such as the North Adams Project. Since 2008, over 1,500 artists have participated in workshops and have received more than $1,600,000 in seed capital funding.

↙ Jenny Holzer, "PROJECTIONS", 2007, light projection, text: "The Terrorist, He's Watching" from "Poems New and Collected": 1957–1997 by Wisława Szymborska.

English translation by Stanisław Barańczak and Clare Cavanagh, © 1998 by Harcourt, Inc. Used/reprinted with permission of the author. © 2007 Jenny Holzer, member Artists Rights Society (ARS), NY, photo: Attilio Maranzano

← Installation view of Sol LeWitt: "A Wall Drawing Retrospective" (on view through 2043)

© Estate of Sol LeWitt/Artists Rights Society (ARS), New York, photo: Zoran Orlić, courtesy MASS MoCA

→ Installation view of Nick Cave: "Until", 2016

Photo: James Prinz, courtesy of the artist and Jack Shainman Gallery, co-produced by MASS MoCA; Crystal Bridges/The Momentary, Bentonville, AK; and Carriageworks, Sydney, Australia

MASS MoCA has initiated numerous cooperations with other cultural institutions to encourage exchange and collaboration. These include partnerships with the Clark Art Institute, the Williams College Museum of Art, and Jacob's Pillow. Additional partnerships with schools are included in the annual program.

The economic consequences following the departure of the factories and the loss of countless jobs in the 1980s can still be felt in the once-booming industrial city of North Adams. Institutions such as MASS MoCA not only contribute to the spread of art and culture; they also ensure the economic recovery of the entire region by creating new jobs and increasing tourist numbers and overnight stays. The objective, therefore, is to expand the synergies between MASS MoCA and the city. Guests are encouraged not only to visit MASS MoCA, but also venture into downtown North Adams to support its local shops, businesses, galleries, cafés, and restaurants and sustainably revitalize the city.

MASS MoCA, however, is much more than a creative and economic force in the region: through its activities, it also promotes a sense of community.

1 Joseph Thompson/Simeon Bruner/John Heon, "From Mill to Museum: Twenty Years of Making Art at MASS MoCA", published by MASS MoCA, 2018, p. 28.

2 MASS MoCA mission statement, available at https://massMoCA.org/about/ (last accessed April 15, 2021).

Cultural Districts: A Brief Typology and Account of Their Significance

by Adrian Ellis

Guggenheim Bilbao
Photo © Image courtesy of FMGB Guggenheim Bilbao Museoa, 2020

They are a global phenomenon. In different parts of the English-speaking world they are referred to variously as "cultural districts", "quarters", "precincts", "hubs", or "clusters"—and "distritos culturales" in Spanish, "distretti culturali" in Italian, "Kulturviertel" in German, "quartiers culturels"in French, "المنطقة الثقافية" (almintaqat althaqafia) in Arabic, and "文化区" (wénhuà qū) in Mandarin. Some districts have existed for decades and even centuries, but, whether old or new, they have in recent decades become the focus of considerable investment and public attention, and organizations have been established to manage them in ways that are intended to advance the agendas of their stakeholders. In short, they have become instruments of urban and cultural policy.

The cultural elements of districts often include one or more anchor institutions that effectively define the area, such as Bilbao's Guggenheim Museum or Tate Modern in London's Bankside. The arts- and culture-related activity is usually mixed in with residential, retail, and office use as well as with public spaces, but the character that the cultural institutions contribute is a critical element in determining who is drawn to the area—whether to live, work, or visit—and in giving the district its overall identity. This is even the case where there is no single predominant cultural anchor. Think of East London's Hoxton or New York's Chelsea, and you will almost certainly think of art galleries: many other things happen there, but the commercial gallery scene is, in a very real sense, globally definitional for these places.

There are many dimensions on which a typology of cultural districts can be mapped. Some districts have long histories dating back decades or in some cases centuries: the Theatre Royal in London's West End theater district, for example, opened in 1663. Berlin's Museumsinsel dates back to 1797. Some districts adhere to a broad masterplan—London's Albertopolis around Exhibition Road was plotted out on land bought with the proceeds of the Great Exhibition of 1851.[1] Others develop organically—"naturally occurring" districts like New York's Fourth Arts Block or Beijing's 798 Art Zone, which is clustered around former military factories. Yet others are considerably more recent and have been built rapidly "top down"—Dallas Arts District, for example, covers 68 acres (27 ha) and contains thirteen performing and visual arts facilities, most of which were completed over a twenty-year period between

1984 and 2004. Hong Kong's 100-acre West Kowloon Cultural District is under phased construction on reclaimed land. Abu Dhabi's Sa'adiyat Island is a similar work in progress, anchored by the Louvre Abu Dhabi, which opened in 2017, and with three other major museums—including the Guggenheim Abu Dhabi and Sheik Zayed National Museum—that are in advanced stages of planning or construction. Often, broadly cultural institutions are collocated with other uses considered synergetic, such as higher education (Sa'adiyat Island again, where New York University's satellite is located, or London's East Bank on London's 2012 Olympic Site, where London College of Fashion and University College London will be joined by Sadler's Wells Dance and an annex of the Victoria and Albert Museum), design (Barcelona's Poblenou District or Design District Helsinki), and entertainment (New York, Times Square).

Another dimension along which differences between cultural districts can be plotted is the range of art forms that they contain: some are specialized, focusing on a single art form (theater districts, museum districts), whilst others host a broad range of cultural uses. Some focus on production (i.e. making, like Poblenou District) and therefore are not primarily public facing, whilst others—Vienna's MuseumsQuartier, for example—lead with cultural consumption (i.e. presenting art to audiences). Most try to combine production with consumption, primarily to create an integrated cultural ecology that embraces all aspects of the cultural supply chain and to encourage creative innovation, but also to give visitors a sense of the texture of the creative process and to give character to the district. This ambition often presents challenges that relate to the different business models and economics of cultural production and consumption.

The extent to which districts are organized formally and the nature of the entities that plan and run them give us another comparative dimension. The models range from lightly articulated coordination to strong central direction by well-funded entities that can also be the landlords of a significant proportion of the real estate (as with The Pittsburgh Cultural Trust in Dubai's Alserkal Avenue). And of course those organizing entities can themselves be private sector, public sector, or non-profit ("third sector") organizations, and their powers can and do vary widely depending upon both the administrative and legal framework under which they are operating and the broader political economy in which they are situated.

Public sector entities are usually charged with the planning and establishment of new districts, usually at arm's length from a central Ministry of Culture or a city agency. But the management of new or established districts can take many organizational forms, the most common of which is some type of non-profit entity. The governance, formal powers, and business model or funding models vary enormously. But the private sector has a significant and growing role in the operation of cultural districts, in part because of the growing use of public-private initiatives in urban development, but also because of developers' quest to find definitional assets to anchor developments in an age when retail is stalling (for example New York's Shed at Hudson Yards).

Better Bankside in London
Photo © Courtesy of Better Bankside, 2020

With so much potential variety across so many dimensions, one might reasonably ask whether there are enough significant commonalities for meaningful comparisons to be made. There are, and over the past six years, the Global Cultural Districts Network has provided a forum for practitioners to compare experiences —both good and bad—and deepen their own understanding of how a complex "place-based cultural ecology" can be created and managed to meet a wider range of policy goals for their stakeholders. The network's success has depended upon there being significant common ground between the members, leading to their wish to compare challenges and opportunities.

Districts—other than those usually small naturally occurring ones with no organizational infrastructure—are purposive: they exist to meet goals and they meet those goals more or less effectively, depending on how much agency they have—that is, what powers—and how well they exercise those powers. The goals of each district—as articulated in their founding charters for example, their strategic plans, or in the contacts they have with their funders and investors—are distinctive. But there is also significant overlap in the types of goals. The ambitions that they are created to promote usually cluster around some subset of the following:

→ Identifying and exploiting economies of scale and synergies between collocated cultural institutions for their collective benefit;
→ Stimulating economic development and innovation, particularly in the creative industries and entertainment;
→ Encouraging tourism by creating an attractive and visible location with critical mass;
→ More generally, promoting the

image of a city or a country—"soft diplomacy"—in the context not just of tourism, but also of encouraging inward investment and attracting knowledge workers;

→ Promoting the health and well-being of residents within a given catchment area;
→ Facilitating social integration and creating "social capital";
→ Enhancing adjacent property values.

The heavily overlapping goals for these purposive entities are what has made the dialogue between districts so rich and rewarding, and it is what makes a discussion of cultural districts as organizational entities valuable: a commonality of ends gives rise to a discussion of appropriate and effective means. However, the policy analysis behind achieving these ends does not yet match the task: the goals of cultural districts are individually complex and indeed sometimes in conflict with each other—for example, raising property values can displace existing communities (gentrification), which is rarely conducive to facilitating social integration, another commonly expressed goal. Many districts aspire to both of these aims.

This agglomeration of complex goals makes the successful establishment and management of cultural districts challenging. Indeed, the fact that these ambitious agendas are often pursued through investment in the arts and in culture is in some ways surprising. Over a thirty-year period, we have moved from cultural policy—and cultural district policy—having the status of an obscure, faintly articulated aspiration held by academics and cultural advocates to cultural policy today being part of the rhetorical framework of practically every city, region, and nation in the world, a framework matched by considerable investment—billions of dollars per annum.[2] Investment in cultural districts—and in their constituent organizations—is a significant part of that broad agenda.

Much of this investment has been driven by variations on the Guggenheim Bilbao theme, some organized around highly sophisticated strategies, built on an understanding of the many dimensions of Bilbao's success: architectural bravura, of course, but also a broader tourist strategy led by regional and local government; public funding to support programming; an astute understanding of the market catchment area (and investment in hotels and transport infrastructure); and the careful management of a synergetic relationship with the local community. Bilbao's first-mover advantage was also significant: Frank Gehry's architecture took advantage of advances in material science, CAD, and structural engineering to become the first of a generation of strikingly expressive architecture. There are now strangely torqued buildings all around the world.

Many cultural strategies, however, are less well thought through than Bilbao's, leading to a more naïve "build and they will come"[3] approach that creates problems of visitation and programmatic quality down the line.For cultural districts to realize their stakeholders' objectives, there are many more factors that need to be taken into account than architectural merit alone.

This focusing of public policy and resources on culture and cultural infrastructure is in some ways paradoxical. The long boom in investment in arts infrastructure over the past three decades does not appear, for the most part, to be demand-led. Audiences and visitors globally for the sort of cultural product that typifies cultural districts have grown, but in mature economies, they have grown more slowly than capacity. The competition for cultural tourists is fierce—cultural tourists stay longer, spend more, and return more often than most other categories of visitors—but there is a "winner takes all" dimension to competition, in which a relatively small number of well-located, high-profile, richly programmed institutions are in a virtuous circle of visitors, financial support (public and private), and investment in assets, while the rest occupy a more challenging environment typified by the sort of plaintive headlines that are always associated with arts funding. Institutions more oriented to a local audience have had to invest more and more aggressively in audience development strategies to cultivate a wider demographic. Success has been mixed.

We need to look at the supply side to understand the main drivers of growth. The most obvious has been globalization: deregulation of financial markets, the dismantling of barriers to free trade and technological innovation creates mobile capital, a mobile workforce of knowledge workers, and mobile high-end tourists. Globalization also generates rapid urbanization. But in the process, it commodifies cities, making them undistinguished and indistinct, offering the same hotels, the same shops, the same brands, and inducing, some would argue, the same sense of bland ennui. If cities are to attract those mobile resources, they therefore need to become attractive brand destinations and magnets for capital—both human and financial. Public safety, education, and transport gets cities so far in the livability ratings, but they also need a well-expressed cultural identity, preferably rooted in some claim for authenticity, or at least that is what many urban planners and leaders have come to believe. Cultural institutions, housed in iconic architecture, have become central to that formula. The sizzle is as important as the steak.

Culture and cultural infrastructure have therefore become important policy tools of strategic place-making, led by the public sector and happily supported by non-profits, with promises of urban regeneration, inward investment, effective management of the "night-time economy" of entertainment and dining, and the creation of social capital—bonds of trust that foster cohesion and well-being. The arts—or at least arts buildings—have a seat at the urban policy table, from Beijing to Riyadh, and from New York to Moscow. The contribution of cultural districts and of the clustering effects of collocating cultural activity has been central to their ascendancy.

However, in parallel with this investment and its rationale, there has also been a drumbeat of concern that the same cultural organizations that in this context are key policy levers also have for some time found themselves facing long-term challenges: changes in demographics and in cultural appetites have meant an emerging mismatch between what they have historically offered and effective demand. This mismatch has been exacerbated by:

Guggenheim Bilbao
Photo © Image courtesy of FMGB Guggenheim Bilbao Museoa, 2020

- → Changes in how people use their leisure time, which is increasingly sliced and diced in ways that the conventions of the performing arts in particular—long-form works at set times—do not easily accommodate;
- → Challenges from vertically integrated entertainment industries that are competing aggressively for people's time and discretionary income—dining, video gaming, home entertainment (Netflix, cable), sport and so on;
- → Challenges from the growth of digital entertainment, which bypasses physical locations beyond a console;
- → Challenges from a desire for greater informality than the sometimes "stuffy" high culture provides and for active participation (co-curation) that is difficult to accommodate within the traditional model of the performing and visual arts.

During this period, the realities of the climate crisis and its environmental and human cost have become apparent to even the most reluctant sensibilities: the cultural sector has been squaring up to its responsibilities for controlling its emissions and educating its audiences as well as to the potential costs of mitigation.

And, in perhaps a final layer of complexity, the recent past has been characterized by growing political polarization in general and the rise of national populism in particular, one result of which has been an intensification of "culture wars" in which the legitimacy and mandate of a wide range of cultural and scientific institutions has been called into question by political leaders, both in opposition and in office. Museums and performing arts organizations in Hungary, Poland, the United States, and Brazil have had their leadership questioned and in some cases their funding revoked in ways that they would not have anticipated in any planning scenarios undertaken a decade ago. There are no reasons to think this trend will subside and many reasons—primarily the polarization of civic discourse—to think it will grow. During the period 2017–2020, appropriate responses to these changes in the operating environment of cultural districts and their constituents all represented the common thread of professional discourse in the cultural sector around the world. These challenges can be summed up in one word: the challenge of "relevance". To work as effective policy instruments in the context of cultural policy in general and cultural district policy in particular, cultural organizations need not just to exist, but to thrive. And to thrive, ultimately, they need to be compellingly relevant to the audiences and visitors, otherwise districts themselves stall, lacking the motor on which they are premised.

The Pandemic

In the autumn of 2020, we are experiencing a prolonged global pandemic that has been responsible for over a million deaths worldwide. The coronavirus pandemic has added an enormous further dimension of complexity to the successful management of cultural districts, as it has to the management of every other sector of the global economy. To fail to acknowledge this would be to fail to acknowledge the most pressing realities of what cultural management or leadership means today. It may be helpful to break down the impact—actual and potential—into its direct and indirect effects.

The direct effect of the pandemic has been effectively to close down large swathes of the cultural sector for a prolonged period. The sector will come back as the pandemic passes, whether the passing is because of effective public health measures (testing and tracing, coherent and enforced distancing policies etc.), because it exhausts itself (the so-called "herd immunity" strategy), or because of the development and distribution of a safe and effective vaccine or palliative. There will therefore be a wide variation between—and in some cases, within—countries with respect to the pace at which this happens, opening up a new dimension of diversity internationally in the context of cultural district management.

There will also be a wide variation in cultural districts' ability to withstand a period of partial closure, depending on:

- → Its duration, which will be subject to wide variation between countries because of variations in public health policy and access to reliable vaccines. The period in which the direct effects are felt will be prolonged in countries where public health policy with respect to the pandemic has been patchy—Britain, the United States, Russia, India, Brazil, and Spain are some of the countries whose struggles to implement effective policies are most manifest.
- → The organizations' circumstances (the extent of financial reserves available to support a period of heavily reduced activity and the ratio of variable costs that can be cut to fixed costs that cannot) and the agility they can muster to leverage digital cultural consumption and related revenue streams;
- → Their ability to apply public health measures (such as social distancing) within the respective district's setting and cultural activities and to re-establish their disrupted cultural supply chains;
- → The extent to which third-party funding (government, philanthropic, and dues) is available to carry organizations through;
- → The degree to which long-haul

tourism—which is anticipated to be subdued for some years[4]—plays a central part in the district's strategy and business model; and

→ The degree to which districts can demonstrate their relevance to the changed circumstances of the communities in which they are based.

Where there is a lack of confidence in public health measures, this will in turn render certain segments of audiences and visitors cautious about returning, including the more affluent and older (and therefore health-conscious) groups that represent the core audience for many forms of traditional cultural products like classical music, theater, and opera. We have already witnessed this in the relatively low attendance of reopened museums in the UK and the USA after the first wave. How long this "social scarring" will endure is unclear, but it is likely to be higher where there is less confidence in public health measures.

There is also a differential impact of the pandemic on different forms of cultural activity that needs to be taken in account. Social distancing, for example, is easier for museums, both front and back of house, than it is for theaters and concert halls, where pinch points in lobbies, on stage, and backstage make it much more difficult to have effective distancing, and where social distancing has an immediate impact on the box office. America's largest performing arts organization, the Metropolitan Opera, has announced its closure until autumn 2021. It favors outdoor programming where distancing is more practicable and for which district managers often have a specific remit.

The indirect effects of the pandemic are no less profound. The most obvious has been to accelerate the trends already in evidence. In addition to the socio-demographic and behavioral trends noted above, five stand out from research and interviews:

→ The closure of physical infrastructure has forced cultural institutions to accelerate their investment in online content to maintain their engagement with their audiences—virtual audiences divorced from physical location, or at least with an episodic relationship with it, will become more important both to mission and, as business models evolve, to the bottom line.

→ The international outcry following the recording and dissemination on social media of the death of George Floyd at the hands of police in Minneapolis in May 2020 added momentum to a wave of impatience at the pace of progress in cultural institutions with respect to racial equity in many countries, particularly but not exclusively English-speaking ones. This put considerable pressure on boards and management to make progress on diversity, equity, access and inclusion—often abbreviated to DEAI—with respect to staffing, programming, and governance at a pace they find challenging.

→ More generally, social media has been used effectively in the cultural sector to draw attention to actual or perceived ethical shortcomings—appropriate board affiliations, appropriate sources of sponsorship and philanthropy, appropriate pay differentials—subjecting many

1 The Great Exhibition of the Works of Industry of All Nations took place in Hyde Park, London, and was the first of the World Fairs, exhibitions of culture and industry, which continue to this day as World Expos (Milan 2015, Shanghai 2010). Dubai's Expo 2020 has been rescheduled to 2021 due to the Covid-19 pandemic.

2 See AEA Consulting's annual review of cultural infrastructure investment, available at https://wfly.co/Fd1OL (last accessed March 29, 2021).

3 "Build and they will come" is often used as shorthand for "supply will create its own demand" and is widely thought to be a line in the film "Field of Dreams", but it does not appear either in the film or the book on which it was based. The line "Build and he will come" does, referring to the protagonist's father.

4 See, for example, the IMF's projections, available at https://www.imf.org/external/pubs/ft/fandd/2020/12/impact-of-the-pandemic-on-tourism-behsudi.htm (last accessed March 29, 2021).

5 See World Bank, "Global Outlook: Pandemic, Recession: The Global Economy in Crisis", 2020, available at https://elibrary.worldbank.org/doi/abs/10.1596/978-1-4648-1553-9_ch1 (last accessed March 31, 2021).

789 Arts District,
Beijing, China
Photo © Pixattitude, Dreamstime.com (license = stock photo with royalty-free license)

boards and management to a level of public scrutiny that is new to them and—at least in the short term—discomforting.

→ The pressure to make savings to minimize operating costs during a period of low programmatic activity has and will continue to present strategic, operational, positioning, and indeed moral dilemmas for management. Staff who are in the front line for furloughs and layoffs are either in front-of-house positions—and therefore statistically often more likely to be minorities—or "creatives" responsible for programming who are as often working under contract as full time salaried staff. Organizational survival may therefore be at odds with moral imperatives, public relations positioning, and the long-term stewardship of creative and technical skills for the sector.

→ The pandemic is precipitating a deep global recession of historic proportions that will exacerbate all these pressures.[5]

Thus the pandemic and its attendant furies have added an important dynamic to cultural district policy and management. The silver lining is thin and modest: the pandemic will incontrovertibly challenge districts and their constituents to address more urgently and perhaps more imaginatively issues that had until now been chronic or long term in character, rather than—as they are now—acute. There is no single answer to them, but to ignore them is to risk being sidelined in both cultural and civic life. We are entering a period of creative destruction and hopefully of creativity: in programming, in management and operations, and in business models.

Vital cultural institutions are necessary but not sufficient for vital, effective cultural districts, and the long-term challenge at the heart of the cultural districts remains: investment in them as policy instruments only pays off if they work their strategic magic with respect to their impact. That strategic magic requires not just compelling architecture and welcoming public spaces, but vibrant institutions generating programming—exhibitions, concerts, experiential events, and so on—that engage audiences and command critical and civic attention.

The discussion in this chapter is explored more fully in "Cultural Districts in Context" by Adrian Ellis and Beliz B. Tecirli (forthcoming 2022).

Museumsinsel Berlin

The Acropolis of Athens on the Spree

by Erwin Uhrmann

The Museumsinsel Berlin is a nineteenth-century museum complex in the center of Berlin between the River Spree and the Spree Canal. It comprises six museum buildings and public gardens. Its museums house eight different collections whose art and cultural history spans over 6,000 years, from antiquity to the twentieth century. The Museumsinsel Berlin was declared a UNESCO World Heritage Site in 1999.

Location	Germany, Berlin, various locations/in the northern part of Spree Island in the historic center of Berlin
Opened	19th century
Total area	8.6 ha (approx. 80,600 m^2)
Number of cultural facilities	6
Leisure facilities & activities	cafés/restaurants, museum shops, bookshops
Visitors/year	3.1 million
Architecture	Karl Friedrich Schinkel, Friedrich August Stüler, Johann Heinrich Strack, Ernst Eberhardt von Ihne, Alfred Messel, Ludwig Hoffmann, David Chipperfield, Julian Harrap, Heinz Tesar, Heinz Hilmer, Oswald Matthias Ungers, Kleihues + Kleihues, HG Merz
Website	www.museumsinsel-berlin.de

History and Architecture

In the Middle Ages, the northern part of Spree Island—the location of today's Museumsinsel—was a marshy wetland. In the thirteenth century, Cölln, Berlin's sister city, began to form on the island's higher, southern part. In the fifteenth century, Elector Friedrich II of Brandenburg built Berlin Palace in the middle of the island. Two hundred years later, the left arm of the Spree was developed into a canal. The marshland was drained, and a pleasure garden for the palace created in its place. After only a short time, the garden's Pomeranzenhof, an orangery where tropical fruits, decorative trees, and ornamental plants were cultivated, was removed to make way for the ramparts built as part of the city's fortifications. Friedrich Wilhelm I had the garden levelled and turned into a military parade ground. The former orangery was relocated and repurposed as the Neuer Packhof, a warehouse used for the interim storage of goods that were traded by ship, such as flour and salt, to relieve some of the burden on the Alter Packhof in nearby Friedrichswerder, which had become too small. When the Neuer Packhof itself reached the limits of its capacity, the architect and master builder Karl Friedrich Schinkel was commissioned to build an extension.

In 1822, Schinkel presented a plan for the redesign of the northern part of Spree Island. The idea of housing the royal art collections in a public museum had already been discussed at the end of the previous century, with the Musée Français at the Louvre in Paris serving as a model. Eventually, Schinkel was commissioned to build the museum, a project aligned with the ideas of the earlier Prussian reforms with which King Friedrich Wilhelm III had initiated a temporary departure from absolutism, laying the foundations for a modern nation state. The museum

↖ Previous double page: Kolonnadenhof, Bodestraße

↓ Altes Museum, Am Lustgarten

← Bode-Museum, Am Kupfergraben

→ The small Dome of the Bode-Museum

↘ Neues Museum, Bodestraße

Photos © Staatliche Museen zu Berlin / David von Becker

was intended to symbolize citizens' freedom and equality with the ruler within the urban fabric. The commission for its construction was led by Wilhelm von Humboldt, brother of the explorer Alexander von Humboldt. In 1830, the Royal Museum (today's Altes Museum) was opened as the first public museum in Prussia. With an architecture that harks backs to antiquity—a wide atrium, eighteen Ionian columns, a large open staircase, and a central interior dome modelled on the Roman Pantheon—it is considered one of the most important works of European Classicism. Only ten years after its opening, however, the space it offered had already become too small for the growing collections.

Friedrich Wilhelm IV dreamt of building a "sanctuary for art and science", where scientists and artists could exchange ideas and the museum would function as an educational institution based on the Humboldtian model. He produced sketches of his ideas, on the basis of which Friedrich August Stüler, a pupil of Schinkel's, developed the site's basic structure and several of its buildings. Stüler first planned the Royal Prussian Museum (now the Neues Museum), which opened in 1859. It embodied the ideal of the "universal museum", where visitors could stroll through the rooms and, as it were, through the art and science of mankind.

Wilhelm's "sanctuary" was originally supposed to have a central temple-like assembly hall to serve as a forum for discourse. During the planning process, the banker and consul Joachim Heinrich Wilhelm Wagener bequeathed to the Prussian state his extensive collection of works by Caspar David Friedrich, Karl Friedrich Schinkel and others, on the condition that it be exhibited in a suitable location. Stüler then re-designed the assembly hall as another museum, the National Gallery, to house the new collection.

With the opening of the National Gallery in 1876, the growing cultural district's program became even more diverse: "While the Old Museum was dedicated to the universal spirit of the Enlightenment and the New Museum showed the ordered historical world, the National Gallery is a product of the national unification movement."[1]

Museumsinsel caught on as the area's name in the 1870s. The concept of the "universal museum" was superseded by the individual museums' increasing specialization and the plan to build two further museums in addition to the existing three.

The Wilhelminian Kaiser-Friedrich-Museum (now the Bode-Museum) was built by architect Ernst Eberhardt von Ihne on the triangular plot at the tip of Spree Island. It was conceived by the art historian Wilhelm von Bode, who assembled the collection of sculptures and paintings it would house. Bode, after whom the museum would later be named, became General Director of the Royal Museums in 1905.

In 1897—one year before the Kaiser-Friedrich-Museum was built—construction began on the Pergamonmuseum. It was opened in 1901 but proved too small to house the archaeological finds from Miletus, Priene, Babylon, Uruk, Egypt, and Assur; it was also found to have several structural defects and was demolished after only seven years. Wilhelm von Bode drafted a new design with sufficient space to accommodate the ancient architecture; he also proposed that the new building house a German Museum devoted to national art history. The planning was undertaken by Alfred Messel and, after Messel's death, by Ludwig Hoffmann. Political upheaval and world events—such as the outbreak of the First World War, the 1918 November Revolution, and the economic turbulence of the 1920s—delayed construction, and the museum was only completed in 1930 in reduced form. At that time, only the east wing of the three-wing building was named the Pergamonmuseum: the north wing was the Deutsches Museum and the south the Vorderasiatisches (southwest Asian) Museum. Only in 1958 was the entire building designated the Pergamonmuseum.

Bode-Museum, view from the Spree
Photo © Staatliche Museen zu Berlin/David von Becker

As the collection expanded steadily over the years, new buildings were added in locations outside the Museumsinsel. One of these was the Kunstgewerbemuseum (Arts and Crafts Museum)—now the Martin-Gropius-Bau—built in Kreuzberg in the 1870s. Bode had also planned a museum complex in Berlin-Dahlem, but this was not realized until the second half of the twentieth century.

Most of the buildings on the Museumsinsel were destroyed in the Second World War. Berlin Palace, parts of which were destroyed by fire, was demolished in 1950. With the division of Berlin, the collections, which had been stored elsewhere during the war, were torn into two arbitrary halves: in East Germany, they were moved into the State Museums; in West Germany, they were housed in the Prussian Cultural Heritage Foundation. In consequence, new art institutions and museum complexes were established in West Berlin, such as the Kulturforum near Potsdamer Platz, the Neue Nationalgalerie, and the museum center in Berlin-Dahlem.

Gradually, the buildings of the Museumsinsel in East Berlin were rebuilt. The most severely damaged of these, the Neues Museum, remained a ruin under constant threat of demolition until just before reunification when, finally, the foundation stone for its reconstruction was laid.

The collections that had been separated after the war were eventually brought back together following Germany's reunification. In 1990, the museum directors from Berlin's former east and west authored a "Memorandum on the future locations and the structure of the National Museums in Berlin", in which they considered the reorganization of the then fourteen individual museums and collections into seven locations, of which the Museumsinsel would be the core site.

In 1993 and 1994, an international architecture competition for the new design of the Neues Museum was held. The commission was ultimately awarded to the architect David Chipperfield together with the restoration specialist Julian Harrap. The substance and historical elements of the original building were preserved or restored. Chipperfield sought a contemporary formal language for the sections that had been completely destroyed while remaining within the cubature originally defined by Stüler.

A team was assembled to plan the renovation of the other museums. It included international architects such as Heinz Tesar for the Bode-Museum and Heinz Hilmer and Christoph Sattler for the Altes Museum.

The Museumsinsel Berlin was declared a UNESCO World Heritage site in 1999. In the same year, the Prussian Cultural Heritage Foundation implemented the "Museumsinsel Master Plan", which set out how the collections would be reorganized and the entire museum ensemble structurally combined and renovated in a manner appropriate to its listed building status. The original concept of creating a "sanctuary for art and science" served as the Master Plan's historical basis.

Alte Nationalgalerie, Bodestraße
Photo © Staatliche Museen zu Berlin/David von Becker

The Master Plan also included the creation of the Archaeological Promenade, an underground passage connecting the Altes Museum, Neues Museum, Pergamonmuseum, and Bode-Museum. A new entrance building for the whole of the Museumsinsel would direct the flow of visitors and ease pressure on the listed structures. Chipperfield had already envisaged such a building in his design for the Neues Museum, and in 2000 he received the commission to realize it. After a protracted period of replanning, the James-Simon-Galerie was finally built and opened in 2019. It is named after James Simon, a Wilhelmine-era Berlin arts patron and entrepreneur who donated the sculpted portrait of Nefertiti—one of the Museumsinsel's best-known pieces—to the Egyptian Museum.

In 2001, the Alte Nationalgalerie was the first building to reopen following restoration. This was followed in 2006 by the completely refurbished Bode-Museum and in 2009 by the Neues Museum, which was renovated in keeping with its status as a listed building and partially completed. The Pergamonmuseum will be given a fourth wing on its originally open side facing the Kupfergraben.

The publicly accessible areas between the museums were redesigned as recreational spaces. The central Colonnade Courtyard, which opened in 2010 and can be traced back to an idea of Friedrich Wilhelm Schinkel, was designed by Levin Monsigny Landschaftsarchitekten as a public garden based on historical models.

Structure

The Museumsinsel Berlin is located in the district of Berlin-Mitte. The roughly triangular peninsula lies between the Spree and the Spree Canal and is connected to the surrounding parts of the city by six bridges. At the northern end of the Lustgarten, the Altes Museum sits diagonally opposite Berlin Cathedral. Behind it runs Bodestraße, which connects with the surrounding area on the Kupfergraben side via the Eiserne Brücke and with the Spree side via the Friedrichsbrücke. The central part of the Museumsinsel consists of the Neues Museum, the Pergamonmuseum, the Alte Nationalgalerie, the Colonnade Courtyard, and the James-Simon-Galerie, which now serves as the newly created main entrance and location of the visitor center, a shop, and a restaurant. A railway bridge separates the Bode-Museum from the rest of the area. Its main entrance is reached via the nineteenth-century Monbijou Bridge at the northern tip of the island. The entire site comprises a total area of 8.6 ha, with the Colonnade Courtyard covering 12,900 m². The outdoor areas are accessible around the clock. Thanks to its central location, the Museumsinsel can be reached by several means of public transport.

← Pergamonmuseum, Am Kupfergraben
Photo © Staatliche Museen zu Berlin/Maximilian Meisse

→ Pergamonmuseum. Das Panorama, Am Kupfergraben
Photo © Staatliche Museen zu Berlin/David von Becker

Organization

The buildings and collections located on the Museumsinsel Berlin are part of the Staatliche Museen zu Berlin (National Museums in Berlin), which comprise a total of fifteen collections and four institutions. The National Museums belong to the Prussian Cultural Heritage Foundation, which is financed by the Federal Government and the states. A financing agreement regulates how funding is secured. Seventy-five percent of the publicly funded portion of the operating budget is contributed by the Federal Government and twenty-five per cent by the states. Each collection, rather than the individual institutions, is headed by a scientific directorate.

Programming

The Museumsinsel program is based upon the eight collections housed in the site's five museums. The Altes Museum displays the Collection of Classical Antiquities with a permanent exhibit of Greek, Etruscan, and Roman art and culture, as well as the Numismatic Collection. The Neues Museum covers the development of prehistoric and early cultures from the Middle East to the Atlantic and from North Africa to Scandinavia. It exhibits objects from the Egyptian Museum and the Papyrus Collection, the Museum of Prehistory and Early History, and the Collection of Classical Antiquities. Its most prominent piece is the portrait bust of Nefertiti. The Alte Nationalgalerie is the main building of the National Gallery collection and exhibits works from the nineteenth and early twentieth centuries. The other parts of the collection are shown in five of Berlin's other museums, including the Neue Nationalgalerie.

The Pergamonmuseum was built primarily to display reconstructions of ancient architecture, including the Pergamon Altar, the Market Gate of Miletus, the Ishtar Gate and Processional Way from Babylon, and the Mshatta Façade. Today, the Pergamonmuseum also houses the Collection of Classical Antiquities, the Museum of the Ancient Near East, and the Museum of Islamic Art.

The Bode-Museum exhibits the Sculpture Collection and houses the Museum of Byzantine Art, but also draws on the collection of the Gemäldegalerie at Potsdamer Platz and parts of the Numismatic Collection.

← Ishtar Gate in the Pergamonmuseum
Photo © Staatliche Museen zu Berlin/David von Becker

Impact

The Museumsinsel attracts around 3.1 million visitors annually. Created in the nineteenth century as a "sanctuary for art and culture", the area remains in a state of flux today in line with political and social changes. Initially, the Museumsinsel was continuously expanded to accommodate its growing collections. During the period in which it was founded, the former Prussian royal seat developed into a world-class metropolis. All of the Museumsinsel's buildings initially were oriented towards Berlin Palace; this axis only changed at the end of the nineteenth century.

↑ Pergamonmuseum. Das Panorama: the panorama by Yadegar Asisi

→ Alte Nationalgalerie

Mshatta Façade in the Pergamonmuseum
Photo © Staatliche Museen zu Berlin/David von Becker

The key template for the current expansion and content configuration of the Museumsinsel is the "Museum Island Master Plan" adopted by the Prussian Cultural Heritage Foundation in 1999. In addition to the renovation of buildings, new constructions, and the reorganization of the collection holdings, the plan envisages the construction of bridges in several directions. To that end, several initiatives were undertaken and an urban planning competition held. One example is the Museumshöfe project, which plans to create new museum spaces as well as depots, administrative offices, and workshops in the area across from the Bode-Museum on the other side of the Kupfergraben. This part of the city is also the site of the Archaeological Center, designed by harris + kurrle architekten and opened in 2012, which houses the Central Archive of the National Museums in Berlin.

On the Museumsinsel's southern side—the former location of Berlin Palace—the Humboldt Forum was built between 2012 and 2021 to serve as a new museum center. Its design partially replicates Berlin Palace and houses museums including the Ethnologisches Museum and the Museum für Asiatische Kunst of the Staatliche Museen zu Berlin as well as the City Museum. The original "sanctuary" thus now extends beyond the boundaries of the Museumsinsel and into the city along several axes, creating a larger, cohesive cultural district. Through this development, the open spaces between the individual institutions have acquired increasing importance as places for social gatherings, recreation, and relaxation.

1 Nikolaus Bernau, "Museumsinsel Berlin", Berlin 200[illegible], p. 32.

MuseumsQuartier Wien

Baroque Meets Cyberspace

by Irene Preißler

Stone horses' heads, modern museum buildings, art installations, places for relaxation—the MuseumsQuartier is characterized by a wide variety of different uses. What formerly was the Imperial Court Stables now houses around sixty cultural institutions while also serving as a living space in the middle of the city.

Location	Austria, Vienna, Museumsplatz 1/ city center
Opened	2001
Total area	approx. 90,000 m²
Number of cultural facilities	approx. 60 (museums, exhibition and event venues, cultural initiatives, etc.)
Leisure facilities & activities	cafés/restaurants, boules court, miniature golf course/sculpture park
Visitors/year	approx. 4.5 million
Architecture	Johann Bernhard Fischer von Erlach, Leopold Mayr, Laurids und Manfred Ortner (O&O Baukunst), Manfred Wehdorn
Website	www.mqw.at

History

A glance into the past reveals the site's colorful history; the period between the first use of the area and the opening of MuseumsQuartier spans almost three hundred years. The area was originally the site of the imperial poultry farm. When the stables in the city became too small, Emperor Karl VI commissioned the well-known architect Johann Bernhard Fischer von Erlach to build new stables on the poultry farm site. After Fischer von Erlach's death in 1722, the project was continued by his son Joseph Emanuel. The baroque main façade, which was completed by Joseph Emanuel in 1725 and is over 300 m long, can still be seen today.

Over the following centuries the site was subject to repeated expansion and modification. With stables for around 600 horses, riding halls, carriage depots, and living quarters for workers, it developed into one of the largest stables of its time.

One of the most striking additions, still preserved today, is the neoclassical Winter Riding School in the MQ Main Courtyard (today Halle E+G), commissioned by Emperor Franz Joseph I and built in 1850 by architect Leopold Mayr, where riding demonstrations were held. In 1874, an octagonal riding hall was built in the so-called Sattlerhof at the request of Empress Elisabeth, where she took riding lessons.

With the introduction of the automobile at the beginning of the twentieth century, the stables increasingly lost their importance; following the First World War and the resulting collapse of the Austrian monarchy, they closed permanently. From the 1920s the area was used as an exhibition site by the Wiener Messe (Vienna Trade Fair) and became known as the Messepalast (Trade Fair Palace). During the Second World War the buildings were used for propaganda events, and after the war the

↖ Previous double page:
View from the MQ Libelle
Photo © Hertha Hurnaus

↓ Historical view of the
Vienna Court Stables ca. 1720,
engraving after Salomon Kleiner
Photo © ÖNB Vienna, Vues III 38034

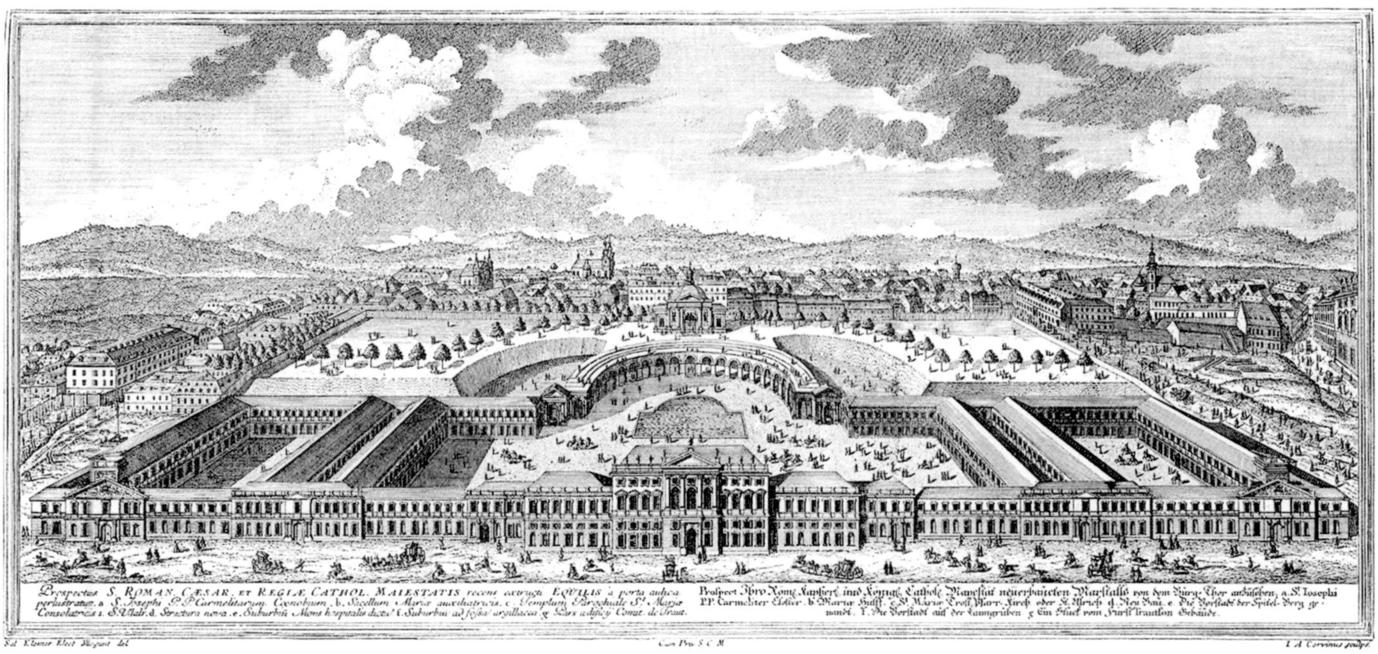

MuseumsQuartier Wien, Main Courtyard
Photo © Hertha Hurnaus

site's function as a location for trade fair activities resumed. Two new large halls were built in the main courtyard to supply additional space. Nevertheless, the premises eventually became too small. Discussions about repurposing the site began in the 1980s. Proposals ranged from a shopping center to a hotel or residential complex; ultimately, it was decided to use the area for cultural purposes.

The first stage of an architectural competition was announced in 1986; following the second stage, the design by brothers Laurids and Manfred Ortner was selected and recommended for implementation in 1990. Protracted political wrangling and protests by residents, however, led to the scaling down of the original design. The ground was finally broken in 1997, and in 2001 the MuseumsQuartier was officially opened.

Planned purely as an arts complex, the focus was to be on the experience of visiting the cultural institutions; use of the outdoor areas was not envisaged. After the historic Fischer von Erlach wing was renovated in 2002, the quartier21 (today Q21) was added as a creative workspace for various initiatives, associations, agencies, and editorial offices. Visitors increasingly complained, however, that the site felt rather lifeless. The director at the time, Wolfgang Waldner, then commissioned the artist Josef Trattner to design giant foam objects for the MQ courtyards.

This proved a successful idea, for the public used the foam shapes enthusiastically in a variety of ways. Subsequently, architects were invited to come up with ideas for courtyard furniture. The concept proposed by the architectural team PPAG (Anna Popelka and Georg Poduschka) was selected. PPAG's furniture, called "Enzis", was first placed in the courtyards in winter 2002 in the form of igloos, and in the following summer as relaxed seating.

With the addition of the courtyard furniture, the MuseumsQuartier gained a new dimension. Suddenly, it was no longer only a venue for viewing art or a space for creative artists; rather, it had become a public gathering place, a place of encounter and exchange, or somewhere people could go simply to have a nice time. Accordingly, the catering on offer was gradually expanded with the addition of restaurants and cafés.

At the same time, the aim still was for the courtyards to promote art, and ensuring easy access to culture was made a priority. Since then, in addition to the programs run by the various cultural institutions, the courtyards have featured free-to-attend artistic events throughout the year.

Under the initiative of MQ director Christian Strasser, plans to offer visitors even more space in the future were revealed to the public in 2014 with the announcement of the MQ Libelle (MQ Dragonfly), a roof structure with a publicly accessible terrace, to be built on top of the Leopold Museum. Construction began in 2018, and, after building works lasting nearly two years, the first major extension of the MuseumsQuartier opened in 2020.

The MQ has continued to be in a constant state of change since its beginnings as the imperial stables.

Architecture

Developed within a revitalized ensemble of baroque buildings, the MuseumsQuartier contains a wide variety of architecture distributed over an area of 90,000 m^2. By virtue of the numerous alterations and extensions in the eighteenth and nineteenth centuries, even the old buildings have evolved through a wide range of construction phases.

Most striking, however, are the three large new buildings in the main courtyard of the MQ (Kunsthalle Wien, Leopold Museum, mumok—Museum moderner Kunst Stiftung Ludwig Wien). As part of Laurids and Manfred Ortner's conception for the development of the site into the MuseumsQuartier, these buildings in particular demonstrate the interplay between the area's historical and contemporary architecture.

The sharp cube of the Leopold Museum, clad in light shell limestone, and the anthracite-colored basalt façade of the mumok with its rounded edges and curved roof were deliberately designed to form a contrast. While the Leopold Museum's exhibition rooms are grouped around a large atrium, combined with windows that flood the rooms on the upper

↑ The MQ Libelle MuseumsQuartier Wien on top of Leopold Museum
Photo © CityCopterCam

↓ View of the MQ Libelle in the MuseumsQuartier Wien on top of Leopold Museum
Photo © Hertha Hurnaus

floors with light, the mumok has only narrow window openings; the two basement and three upper floors are connected by a continuous open space 41 m high. The staircase entrances to both museums stand at a height of 4 m, softening the rising terrain towards the city's seventh district. In contrast, the Kunsthalle Wien is clad in red brick. It is located alongside the historic Winter Riding Hall, today's Halle E+G, with which it shares a common foyer. Apart from small window openings, its design deliberately does away with natural light sources.

Architect Manfred Wehdorn was responsible for overseeing the renovation and adaptation of the listed buildings. The installations in the old baroque buildings were designed by young Austrian architects among others, who emphasized and took into account the buildings' historical substance.

The MQ Libelle, designed by Laurids Ortner (Ortner & Ortner Baukunst), is a structure on the roof of the Leopold Museum that "airily floats like a butterfly … with its wings over the stony cube of the Leopold Museum",[1] and includes a publicly accessible terraced landscape. Two Austrian artists also contributed to the project. Eva Schlegel's work "veiled" is draped around the glass façade of the building like a gossamer silk cloth. In the terrace area, "Lichtkreise" (Circles of Light) by Brigitte Kowanz creates an ambient atmosphere.

Organization

The MuseumsQuartier site is owned by the Republic of Austria. The MuseumsQuartier Errichtungs- und Betriebsgesellschaft (MQ E+B) is a private organization under the leadership of a managing director. Seventy-five percent of the MQ E+B is owned by the Republic of Austria and twenty-five percent by the City of Vienna. Rental agreements are in place with the individual institutions. The Q21 is a division of MQ E+B; the fifty or so cultural initiatives located at the Q21 have direct two-year contracts with MQ. The intent is to create a dynamic structure to complement the new, permanent cultural institutions. Hence, all cultural institutions in the MQ are autonomous and have their own organizational structures.

The MQ E+B is responsible for maintaining the entire complex and its buildings, as well as for the use of and programming in the outdoor areas. In addition, the shop MQ Point also serves as a central information and ticket sales point.

Maintenance and operating costs are financed through subsidies provided by the Republic of Austria and the City of Vienna. Cultural programs are funded through the rental of event spaces, income from ticket sales, and shop revenue. Some individual projects are also supported through sponsorship. The individual institutions receive subsidies from the Republic of Austria or the City of Vienna; the Leopold Museum is a private foundation.

Structure

The MuseumsQuartier is located in Vienna's seventh district and borders the edge of the first district across from the Kunsthistorisches Museum and the Naturhistorisches Museum. A self-contained area, it is bordered on three sides by the shopping street Mariahilfer Strasse, by Breite Gasse, and by Burggasse, and on the front by Museumsplatz. The site is served by eight separate entrances, each accessible around the clock, with no entry fee. The individual cultural institutions each have their own opening hours and admission prices.

Programming

With around sixty cultural institutions, cafés and restaurants, seating furniture and recreational facilities, the MuseumsQuartier is a center of diversity. The new, permanent cultural institutions and fifty cultural initiatives located in the Q21 space offer a spectrum ranging from visual and performing arts to architecture, dance, music, fashion, theater, literature, children's culture, game culture, street art, design, photography, and much more.

Austria's museum of architecture, Architekturzentrum Wien, reveals in its permanent overview and international themed exhibitions how architecture and urban planning shape the daily lives of all people. The museum also organizes workshops, lectures, guided tours, city expeditions, and film series.

Dschungel Wien—Theater for Young Audiences is a center for children, families, and young adults, offering a wide range of performances, from dance to drama, narrative theater, object and puppet theater to opera and music theater, as well as interdisciplinary theatrical forms.

In addition to the events in the Wiener Festwochen and Tanzquartier Wien, the Halle E+G serves as the venue for many concerts and theater and dance productions.

The Kunsthalle Wien is focused on the role that art plays in the process of social change. In addition to producing exhibitions, the Kunsthalle conducts research on artistic practices and supports local and international artists.

The Leopold Museum houses the comprehensive collection of late nineteenth-century and modernist art founded by Rudolf Leopold. It comprises more than 6,000 items and includes the world's largest collection of works by the Austrian Expressionist Egon Schiele, as well as other works of Viennese modernism and the Arts and Crafts of the Wiener Werkstätte.

The comprehensive collection of international twentieth and twenty-first century art at the mumok—Museum moderner Kunst Stiftung Ludwig Wien ranges from classical modernism to pop art, Fluxus, Nouveau Réalisme, and Viennese Actionism.

MuseumsQuartier Wien, Main Courtyard
Photo © Alexander Eugen Koller

The program of Tanzquartier Wien (TQW) includes premieres by Austrian artists and guest performances of international productions. The TQW also offers daily training and regular workshops to professional dancers.

WIENXTRA-Kinderinfo provides information about children's culture and leisure activities in Vienna for children up to thirteen years of age.

The ZOOM Children's Museum offers a hands-on exhibition, various play and adventure areas, as well as four different areas featuring hands-on programs for children up to fourteen years old.

The range offered by the museums and exhibition spaces is complemented by the fifty or so cultural initiatives based at Q21. These cover a wide variety of fields, from international film and dance festivals, indie game development, digital culture, art book publishing and fashion shops. The frei_raum Q21 exhibition space presents temporary group exhibitions with free admission.

Culture is not to be found only in the various galleries and spaces, but also in the outdoor areas. In cooperation with the MQ institutions or external partners, numerous art projects and cultural and leisure events are programmed in the outdoor areas throughout the year. These include classical music concerts, readings, film festivals, pop concerts, performances, sculptures, and installations.

The nine themed passages in the MuseumsQuartier also present art in the public space. The site is criss-crossed by several passages that originate in the MuseumsQuartier's history as the Imperial Court Stables. Some of these passages have been converted into "micro-museums", each dedicated to a different genre of art, such as sound art, comic art, street art, typography, literature, photography, performance, and visual art. In addition to the permanent ceiling designs by contemporary artists, the passages also feature exhibitions programmed by external curators.

This exchange between inside (the museums, exhibitions, and event venues) and outdoors (the courtyards and the forecourt) can kindle visitors' curiosity to explore the programs of the institutions, and can work to break down barriers to art and culture.

Q21's Artist-in-Residence program focuses on networking and exchange. The cultural initiatives at Q21 invite international guest artists to live and work in studios on the grounds for one to two months or to realize projects on site. The support of the respective cultural initiatives allows artists-in-residence to benefit from their direct proximity to the local cultural scene, which in turn allows those initiatives to expand their international reputation and networks.

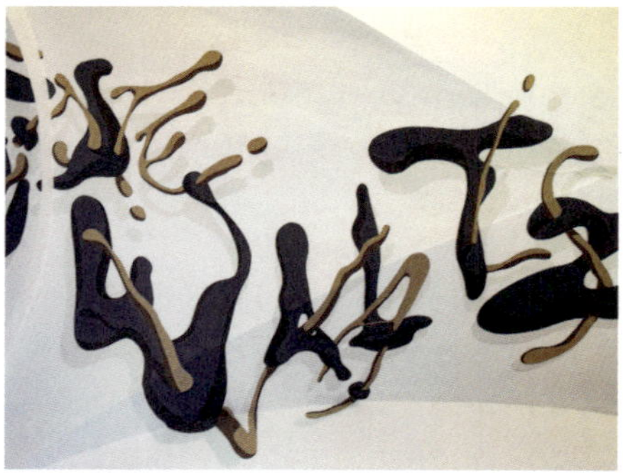

← MuseumsQuartier Wien
Typopassage, micro museum for design

→ MuseumsQuartier Wien
Sternenpassage ("star passage")
Photos © eSeL.at - Lorenz Seidler

← MuseumsQuartier Wien, open air concert by the Vienna Philharmonic
Photo © eSeL.at/Lorenz Seidler

→ MuseumsQuartier Wien, Literature Festival O-TÖNE
Photo © Eva Ellersdorfer-Meissnerova

Impact

As a cultural metropolis, Vienna is known above all for its imperial cultural heritage. With the mix of historical and contemporary elements, both in terms of its architecture and cultural programming, the MuseumsQuartier reveals a lesser-known facet of the city and so adds to the appeal that Vienna holds for tourists. Of the approximately 4.5 million annual visitors to the MuseumsQuartier, twenty percent are international guests, ten percent come from the Austrian provinces, and seventy percent from Vienna itself.

The MuseumsQuartier is thus a meeting place for the Viennese and a place for relaxation in the center of the city. The MQ courtyard furniture provides seating that is free for visitors to enjoy, and there is no compulsion to purchase anything or visit any of the institutions. This holds true also for the MQ Libelle on the roof of the Leopold Museum, opened in 2020, with its view over Vienna's city center. The Libelle was deliberately conceived to be an additional facility available to everyone, offering the opportunity for interaction and dialogue. The MuseumsQuartier, then, contributes not only to Vienna's cultural impact, but also to improving quality of life.

The artists who live and work on site throughout the year also create a cosmopolitan and creative climate. This not only encourages international networking, but also has an impact on the local cultural scene. A multitude of galleries and creative offices have sprung up in the area around the MuseumsQuartier since it opened, especially in Vienna's seventh district, which has helped to transform the image of the area.

As much as the MuseumsQuartier radiates outward, the relative insularity of its architecture also conveys a feeling of safety and security; ideas can form and be discussed in a "protected" space before they are brought out to the open, which in turn creates a sense of freedom.

1 https://ortner-ortner.com/de/baukunst/projekte/kultur/mumok_wien (last accessed April 4, 2021)

Poblenou District

Creative Industry Instead of Smoking Chimneys

by Irene Preißler

Poblenou District is not a cultural district in the narrow sense, but a neighborhood of Barcelona where there is a concentration of cultural, creative, and economic as well as recreational and domestic activities and enterprises. Part of the administrative district of Sant Martí, together with the 22@ project it is known as a center for technology and innovation, as well as for the diversity of its cultural and creative facilities and institutions.

Location	Spain, Barcelona, El Poblenou, Sant Martí/city outskirts
Opened	beginning of the 19th century (Poblenou), from 1992 (22@innovation district project)
Total area	Poblenou neighborhoods: Poblenou: 154.5 ha Provençals de Poblenou: 110.5 ha Poblenou 22@ Innovation District project: 200 ha
Number of cultural facilities	no actual number provided, due to being an urban district; cultural facilities, cultural institutions and creative facilities, technology and innovation center
Leisure facilities & activities	cafés/restaurants, residential units, shops, etc.
Visitors/year	n/a, due to being an urban district
Architecture	a wide variety of architects due to the large number of facilities
Website	www.poblenouurbandistrict.com www.22network.net

History and Architecture

The former marshland on which Poblenou District is located today was used for agricultural purposes until the eighteenth century. Its proximity to the city and its seaside location with open access to the water sparked a veritable boom of factory building with the advent of industrialization at the beginning of the nineteenth century. This increased the demand for skilled labor, which in turn led to rapid population growth.

The area was known colloquially as "Pueblo Nuevo", or "Poble Nou" in Catalan. In its architecture, it follows the fundamental principles of Ildefons Cerdà, the great nineteenth-century Barcelonan city planner, who expanded the city through a grid structure, still known today as l'Eixample.

The completion of the Passeig del Cementiri in 1893 provided a direct connection to Barcelona and, in 1848, a connection with Spain's first railway, so that by the 1870s the number of factories had again proliferated, earning Poblenou the nickname of Catalan Manchester. Sant Martí became a district of Barcelona as part of an extensive incorporation of municipalities in 1897.

From the early 1950s onwards, Spain's weak economy saw numerous companies go bankrupt, more than 1,300 factories close down, and thousands of workers become unemployed. With the departure of industry and residents, the district's slow decline began.

↑ Poblenou District
Photo © Pavel Adashkevich/Shutterstock

↖ Previous double page:
Poblenou District
Photo © Courtesy Poblenou Urban District

The revitalization of Poblenou District began in 1992, when Barcelona hosted the Olympic Games. The building of numerous roads gave Poblenou District excellent connections to the city center, port, and airport. The district was also completely renovated and redesigned, with the Olympic Village and Olympic Port built on the former railway line. The completion of Diagonal Avenue in 1999 established a direct link to downtown Barcelona, the city's financial center.

These new developments triggered a public debate on how to redesign the approximately 200-ha former industrial site. This brought about the adoption in 2000 of the Amended Metropolitan Master Plan, better known as the 22@Plan, which envisaged transforming the old factory buildings in the eastern part of the city and the industrial site into a new urban center for innovation and creativity.

The plan set out three objectives: revitalization of the old factory buildings for economic, social, or leisure activities; economic revival and development into a world-class scientific, technological, and cultural center; and social regeneration through the networking of companies,

Disseny Design Museum and Torre Agbar in Barcelona
Photo © Axel Bueckert, Dreamstime.com

institutions, residents, and cultural and educational facilities. A total of four million m² of new space was to be created at a cost of approximately €180 million.

At the same time that the plans to make Poblenou Barcelona's new center of technology and innovation got underway, increasing numbers of creatives, artists, and cultural organizations, attracted by the relatively low rental prices, moved into the district's many vacant buildings. Among them was Antoni Miralda, or Mariscal, the founder of the legendary Palo Alto design studio.

The construction of the Teatre Nacional de Catalunya in the early 1990s resulted in the Glòries project, as part of which it was resolved to create further cultural institutions to attract more visitors to Poblenou District. These included the Teatre Nacional de Catalunya, L'Auditori—Museu de la Música, the Escuela Superior de Música de Catalunya (ESMUC), and the Disseny Hub de Barcelona. With this growth and development, Poblenou District has developed from a former industrial area into an innovative and creative urban quarter.

Organization

The city's 22@Coordination Commission has managed the district since 2017. Its aim is to position Barcelona as an economic metropolis and center of innovation. Social, sustainable, and innovative aspects are thus the principal areas of focus.

The district's media sector, led by the Barcelona Media Innovation Center (Barcelona Media 2012) and Barcelona Media Park, is a cooperation between the City of Barcelona, Pompeu Fabra University, and the company MediaPro. Their objective is to enhance networking between businesses and private and public institutions. Cultural institutions are promoted by the Ajuntament de Barcelona and the Generalitat de Catalunya.

Purely private organizations also play an important role. Poblenou Urban District, for example, was founded in 2012 by companies in the creative sector in order to pool the district's cultural activities and attractions. Poblenou Urban District has over 140 members, from galleries and museums to creative centers, cultural institutions, working spaces, and hubs. It is organized by a general assembly, which comprises the association's members and meets once a year, and by a board of representatives from each sector. Financing is provided by member contributions, public subsidies, cooperations, and sponsoring.

Structure

Poblenou District is a neighborhood in Barcelona's Sant Martí district (formerly Sant Martí de Provençals), one of the city's ten political and administrative districts. It stretches from the lower part of the old town through Ciutat Vella and l'Eixample to the river Besòs. Poblenou District is home to numerous cultural and creative institutions, as well as to technology companies, housing, cafés, restaurants, and leisure facilities.

- Art galleries, museums, and showrooms
- Creative centers and artists' studios
- Higher education centers for design and architecture
- Design and architecture studios
- Communication and advertising agencies
- Production studios and events
- Co-working centers and hubs
- Foundations and associations
- Shops and fashion showrooms
- Concert halls, theaters, and music
- Printing houses and industrial services
- Leisure and wellness
- Restaurants and delicatessen
- Hotels and hostels

Map & Guide AW21
Biannually publication created by the private association Poblenou Urban District.

Poblenou District, Open Night, 2015
Photo © Courtesy Poblenou Urban District

→ Design Day, 2017,
Poblenou District
Photo © Courtesy Poblenou Urban District

↓ Palo Alto Market,
Poblenou District
Photo © Oriol Alamany/Alamy Stock Foto

Programming

From the outset, the goal has been to establish Poblenou District both as an artistic and creative district and as a center of innovation and contemporary cultural production on an international level. Working to ensure this are organizations such as Poblenou Urban District, whose activities strengthen the synergy between individual cultural and creative institutions and develop cultural attractions and programs.

Public initiatives include Poblenou Open Night and Poblenou Open Day, when all institutions open their doors to the public, who can get to know the district through an extensive program of cultural activities. During Windows Art Circuit, artists fill their displays with sculpture, while Off Llum Bcn takes visitors on a walking tour of light installations curated by Poblenou Urban District.

The site's great variety of art and cultural institutions yields a wide-ranging mix of themes. The larger cultural institutions include the Teatre Nacional de Catalunya (TNC), L'Auditori—Museu de la Música, the Escuela Superior de Música de Catalunya (ESMUC), the Disseny Hub de Barcelona, the Museu del Disseny de Barcelona, and the Can Framis (Museum of Contemporary Catalan Painting).

There are also numerous creative, design, and artists' studios. These include Palo Alto, one of the first institutions to settle in Poblenou District and one of the first to convert a former factory building into a design studio. The electrics company Simon developed the Espacio Simon 100, which feels more like an art gallery than a business enterprise. Likewise located here is La Escosesa, a former industrial complex that has been converted into studios in which artists from a wide range of disciplines live and work. The site is also home to various educational institutions such as the Barcelona Academy of Art, the Barcelona School of Creativity, and the BAU Design School, which offers university courses in design. The area also boasts a multitude of workshops, alternative galleries, film production companies, concert halls, architecture studios, dance clubs, advertising agencies, furniture shops, showrooms, artists' associations, designer hotels, start-ups and much more. Barcelona Media Park, in turn, is the home to a concentration of media production and communication companies, supported by Pompeu Fabra University.

A wide array of companies of varying sizes from the fields of culture, media, and design have come together in Poblenou District. With the 22@ project, a center of technology and innovation was created with the aim of transforming Barcelona into a leading city in the technology sector—a major driver of the Catalan economy—in Europe and throughout the world.

Poblenou District is home to more than 100 small and medium-sized enterprises, as well as a large number of restaurants, hotels, apartments, shops, and other leisure facilities.

Impact

Culture, the creative industries, and cutting-edge technologies are vital to a city's growth, competitiveness, prosperity, and employment opportunities. In Barcelona, 12.6 percent of jobs in the second quarter of 2018 were created by companies in the creative sector.[1]

Cultural activity, though present throughout all of Barcelona, is especially concentrated in two areas of the city. Both El Raval in Barcelona's Old Town and Poblenou District evolved though strategies of urban revitalization and economic development. But while El Raval was advertised as a "cultural district" primarily by the city administration in the mid-1980s, Poblenou District has been shaped by the economic development of businesses in the cultural and creative sectors. This clustering of institutions operating in the same field stimulates joint ventures and reduces costs for the individual players.

The Barcelona Institute of Culture's Creation Factories program, for example, has created locations where young, aspiring artists can find support. They are given the opportunity not only to pursue their art, but also to present their works in the city.

For more than one hundred years, Poblenou District was the most important industrial area of Barcelona and one of the main engines of the Catalan economy. As part of Sant Martí, one of the city's ten political and administrative districts, Poblenou District stretches from the Old Town and the Eixample district to the river Besòs and has experienced a major transformation through the years. The revitalization of its approximately

Poblenou District
Photo © Courtesy Poblenou Urban District

Cloud Nothings band at Parc Central del Poblenou on May 29, 2011 at Primavera Sound Festival
Photo © Christian Bertrand, Dreamstime.com

200 ha aimed to further strengthen the city's position as a green and sustainable area, a "mixed city, which rebalances uses, with environmental quality in a neighbourhood that needs more life, more neighbours",[2] Janet Sanz, deputy mayor and director of the urban planning area, said in 2000.

The entire Sant Martí district thus represents both the past and the future of Barcelona. The formerly agricultural and, later, industrial quarter has become a model for the modernization of a district, a symbol of modern urban planning.

The transformation of this former industrial area into an innovative technological and creative district that features exciting architectural and historical monuments, as well as the conversion of old factory buildings into cultural and creative facilities, has also reconciled the realms of culture and business. The Creativity, Design and Culture Commission was founded within the 22@Network Association, the district's economic body, in order to position 22@District as an ecosystem of culture, creativity, and innovation. Meanwhile, some of the most important cultural and creative institutions have become members of the 22@Network Association in the interest of strengthening the connection of business, technology, and innovation with art, culture, and the creative economy.

Poblenou District, then, stands as an international model for urban, economic, social, and cultural revitalization and innovation.

1 Document "POBLENOU DISTRICT: Barcelona's Innovation, Creative and Cultural District", p. 10

2 Document "POBLENOU DISTRICT: Barcelona's Innovation, Creative and Cultural District", p. 38

On the Urban Function and Cultural Symbolism of Cultural Districts

by Vitus H. Weh

Centre Pompidou Library: Paris's open study room

Photo © Thomas Guignard

Globally, more and more cultural districts are emerging, where different institutions such as museums, theaters, and concert halls come together to form urban ensembles. The experience of a cultural district is no longer just about the classic subject-viewer response. The number of people who visit primarily to use the surrounding grounds is growing faster than the number of visitors to the venues themselves, although these are heavily advertised to the tourism sector.

This is not surprising. Cultural districts offer spatial and social qualities that have otherwise become scarce in cities. At the same time, these heterogenous areas express an appealing socio-political symbolism.

The well-known museums in large cities such as Amsterdam, Paris, London, or Vienna—a pandemic notwithstanding—are visited by millions of people every year. A high share of these, usually between seventy and ninety percent, is made up of domestic and foreign tourists. In some large museums, such as the Belvedere in Vienna or the Louvre in Paris, the share of international visitors alone is over eighty percent. It appears as though the state of "being on foreign soil" and visiting an art museum are a good match: in a foreign country, one is obliged to try new things; when traveling one seeks a change of perspective; on a journey, we also take an interest in things we do not understand.

By implication, however, it follows that many cultural institutions, while a local source of pride—the situation is similar with opera houses and concert halls—are visited surprisingly little by the local population. What is more, the social stratification of visitors is distinctly skewed towards older people and those with university educations.

The visitor statistics of cultural districts tell a completely different story. A cultural district is the spatial and structural grouping of several independent cultural institutions such as museums, concert halls, and theaters into one unified cultural ensemble. Its topography, composition, and size are open. It can take the form of long streets with peripheral buildings, like the National Mall in Washington, D.C., the Museumsufer in Frankfurt, or the Kunstmeile in Krems. It can appear in the form of expansive parks, such as Insel Hombroich near Düsseldorf, Gorky Park in Moscow, or Brazil's Instituto Inhotim. Other districts are clustered around public squares, such as the Museumplein in Amsterdam, Matthäikirchplatz in Berlin, and the Kansalaistori in Helsinki. Some cultural centers breathe new life

← Humboldtforum Berlin: austere from the outside, with passages and intimate courtyards on the inside.

→ Museumplein Amsterdam: From parking lot to green space.

Photos © Vitus Weh

into former royal residences, such as the Hermitage in St. Petersburg, or Vienna's MuseumsQuartier (MQ Wien), which was established in the former court stables. Yet other districts are made up of completely new buildings in what were once run-down neighborhoods, for example Lincoln Center in New York City, whose construction began on the Upper West Side in 1959. They can be large in scale, such as the West Kowloon Cultural District being developed in Hong Kong, or small, like LAC Arte e Cultura in Lugano. In exceptional cases, establishing a cultural district does not even require any new construction. A summarizing name and a logo are sufficient, as with the Kunstareal München.

Nonetheless, one peculiarity remains: while the individual cultural institutions continue to advertise their own content, the concept of a larger "district", "forum" or "center" is communicated at the same time. Moreover, the surrounding open spaces are often used to present a supplementary program. This opens up not only a stronger spatial perspective on cultural institutions, but also a further, urban use for them.

Surveys conducted over several years by MQ Wien show that of its more than four million annual visitors, about seventy percent are Viennese residents, twenty percent come from the other Austrian federal states, and only ten percent are international tourists. Its public is also unusually young: thirty-three percent of the MuseumsQuartier's visitors are aged between twenty and twenty-nine, twenty-six percent are between thirty and thirty-nine, and only eighteen percent are over fifty. The average age is thirty-six.

Even more surprising is the fact that only around fifty percent of all MuseumsQuartier visitors attend any of its numerous exhibitions or events. The remaining fifty percent come for other reasons. In other words, two million visit MQ Wien for no other reason than to meet with other people, to stroll around the traffic-free courtyards, to bask in the sun, to frequent the cafés and restaurants, to recline on the free-to-use courtyard furniture to appreciate the varied architecture or read, or to play minigolf and boccia. The MuseumsQuartier offers spatial, social, and aesthetic qualities unmatched elsewhere in the city.

This operating principle—that of the cultural district as urban oasis—is by no means unique to Vienna. The numerical ratios at the Museumplein in Amsterdam and the area around London's Tate Modern are similar. The Tate Modern, which opened in a former power station, ranks as the most-visited modern art museum in the world. Originally conceived to receive two million visitors per annum, with free admission it now draws six million. In 2006, Vicente Todolí, the Tate Modern's director from 2003 to 2010, described its excessive crowding as "people looking at people looking at people looking at art". A ten-story extension opened in 2016. Todolí's successor, Chris Dercon, urged a positive view of the fifty percent of visitors only interested in the Tate as a meeting place, its spectacular setting, or its free infrastructure: "The new Tate Modern will be so much more than a container for art—it will be a platform for human encounters."

The Museumsufer in Frankfurt am Main and the Centre Pompidou in Paris are considered important, contrasting models of this "mixed cultural use". The Museumsufer in Frankfurt am Main was developed in the 1980s as an urban counterpart to the high-rises of the banking district. Financial Frankfurt was to get a cultural counterpart, so to speak. Existing museums on the south bank of the Main (Weltkulturen Museum, Städel Museum, Liebieghaus) were augmented with adaptations, extensions, and new buildings (Museum Angewandte Kunst, Deutsches Filmmuseum, Deutsches Architekturmuseum, Museum für Kommunikation) to create a unified ensemble. At the same time, the adjacent bank of the Main was transformed into an attractive public leisure area. The spatial interaction at the annual "Museumsuferfest" is particularly celebrated. Over one weekend, around three million visitors stroll past stages, kiosks, and stalls against the backdrop of the river and museums. The museums also offer reduced admission prices, but few people (only around one percent of visitors) take advantage of the opportunity. In comparison, all museums in Frankfurt am Main combined reach a yearly total of around 2.5 million visitors.

The Centre national d'art et de culture Georges-Pompidou in Paris, which opened in 1977, practices its mixed usage

via two separate entrances. From the front, through the main entrance at Place Georges Pompidou, the Centre presents itself as a tourist-friendly exhibition building for modern art (MNAM, Musée National d'Art Moderne), while, via the rear of the building, the local population can visit the admission-free Bibliothèque Publique d'Information (BPI). Both receive roughly the same number of visitors per year (in 2016: MNAM: 1.8m; BPI: 1.5m).

Cultural districts thus usually aim to appeal to a wide range of user groups. In the institutions, the "cultural augmentation" of the classical reception of individual works of art can vary greatly. The spectrum ranges from a spectacular library as a space for urban living (Oodi, Helsinki), fitness equipment and a large skating rink (Gorky Park, Moscow), festivals of light (Quartier des Spectacles, Montréal), and unusual courtyard furniture (MQ Wien) to bustling rows of restaurants (Southbank Centre, London). Generally speaking, it is only through such urban offerings that cultural districts achieve a broad impact. The telling example of the Berliner Kulturforum illustrates that the high quality of content offered by united cultural institutions and the quality of their architecture alone do not automatically result in public acceptance. Despite decades of architectural improvements, the Kulturforum has never become a "cultural ensemble" positively received as a whole. Whether its next addition (Museum der Moderne) will change this remains to be seen.

Experience shows that an ensemble's appeal lies less in artistic or architectural excellence than in social performance and symbolism. Apart from their actual function, public buildings also serve the purpose of collective representation. Through their location, size, and facilities, they aim to create identification and ideational orientation. In this, they are quite literally social role models: both a form of expression of and a starting point for personal and social self-images and awareness. Besides the halls of political power and civic administration, so-called cultural buildings—that is, concert halls, opera houses, theaters, libraries, and museums—are especially important.
In the nineteenth century, these were symbolically charged mostly through their location in the city's central square

← Kulturforum Berlin: Tilted stone terrace as an urban desert.
Photo © Andreas Praefcke, Wikimedia Commons, CC-BY-SA-3.0

→ The picture gallery is only visible from the aerial view.
Photo © Miriam Guterland, Wikimedia Commons, CC-BY-SA-3.0

and the chosen historicist architectural style. For example, a neo-Gothic town hall spoke of public spirit and clarity, a neo-baroque building of dignity and the claim to power; an entrance adorned with Attic columns evoked democratic ideals, whereas a neo-Renaissance façade spoke of a mercantile attitude. Often the reference was made even clearer with sculpted figures or dedicatory inscriptions on the façade. Since the onset of modernity, however, architectural symbolism has been conveyed principally through the iconic character of the design, the interior and exterior spatial program, the materials used, and the embedment in an ensemble. Cultural districts that bring different institutions together under one larger structure have proved to be very powerful instruments of our time.

Here, the assembled spectrum of the institutions and their hierarchal staging are already significant. Historically, the individual cultural sectors have never held an equal footing, whether socially or in their budgetary needs. The theater can lay claim to the longest architectural history. Many impressive amphitheaters have survived from Greek and Roman antiquity. However, theaters were never able to regain their past importance as gathering places for society. The oldest enclosed, permanent theaters of the modern era dated from around 1600 and were much smaller. The opera house then assumed this central function in the second half of the seventeenth century. Although only a recent musical genre, opera quickly achieved cultural and societal supremacy. Its venues were correspondingly opulent and prominently located. The somewhat austere large concert halls, on the other hand, came into fashion at the end of the nineteenth century. The common form of the art museum familiar today also emerged around this time.

All these institutions for the most part are restricted to a very limited canon of works, with dedicated audiences who rarely mix. An opera lover will rarely be found at a contemporary dance performance, a fan of visual art rarely encountered at a design museum, and vice versa. So why bring such contrary worlds together?

The guiding principle that has developed in this regard since the 1950s is that of "culture for all". It was made binding at the second United Nations Convention (CESR: International Covenant on Economic, Social and Cultural Rights), which came into force in 1976.

The rights to work, to well-being, to culture and education, to housing, and to benefit from scientific progress formulated therein are fundamental promises of modernity. Ultimately, the Convention articulates the ideal of an individual and empowered citizen as the nucleus of our democratic society.

← Colorful brownfields: WUK in Vienna
Photo © Wolfgang Thaler

→ The Rote Fabrik in Zurich
Photo © VVPhotography

In the cultural sphere, the central concept of participation led to a massive re-evaluation of popular and everyday culture, working culture, do-it-yourself practices, and oral history from the 1960s onwards. Accordingly, new types of cultural institutions emerged, such as socio-cultural centers, youth art schools, and cultural workshops. They were established mostly in abandoned factory buildings in the periphery. Within the old brick walls of the KOMM in Nuremberg (from 1973), the Arena (from 1976) and WUK (from 1981) in Vienna, and the Rote Fabrik in Zurich (from 1980)—to name but a few examples from the German-speaking world—there emerged a biotope of an alternative concept of culture, one that relied strongly both on the cultural production/self-realization of as many people as possible and on the parallel existence of highly diverse interests. In practice, they clearly demonstrated that the best place for a white exhibition space can be next to a smoky bar, that self-contained artists' studios are in tune with an open bicycle repair shop, and that rehearsal spaces for bands can sit straightforwardly next to a kindergarten, a free school, or the meeting rooms of political groups and social initiatives. In practice, they also showed how it is possible to create cultural and social places that remain lively throughout the day through the staggered use of space, restaurants, open-air cinemas, and courtyard festivals. And so they became an important model for the cultural districts of today.

Drastic changes in the self-conception of the museums themselves likewise pointed the way forward. Today's "art museum" has its origin in historically diverse sources. Traditionally, "museum", referring to the famous Museion ("place of the muses") in ancient Alexandria, was understood as a library. Accordingly, numerous literary reading circles and magazines of the eighteenth and nineteenth centuries called themselves "museums". Europe's first self-contained "museum buildings"—the British Museum in London, opened in 1759, and the Museum Fridericanum in Kassel, opened in 1779—were also libraries first and foremost.

Not until the Museum of the Public in Paris, founded in 1793 and named the Musée Napoléon from 1803 onwards, did the term effectively transfer over to the arts. This was connected to a scientific-encyclopedic requirement that now also came to be applied to old art collections. In Vienna in 1778, a start had already

been made on arranging the imperial collection according to region and school of painting. This still informs contemporary museums' important claim to education and public benefit.

The older tradition, on the other hand, presented art in a "picture gallery". The term "gallery" comes from the Italian word "galleria" and means an elongated walkway between buildings. Galleries have been used to exhibit paintings since the sixteenth century. The famous Galleria degli Uffizi in Florence has existed since 1580. The Grande Galerie in Paris was built from 1595 to 1608 as a passageway connecting the Palais du Louvre and the Palais des Tuileries. The first independent picture galleries opened in Salzdahlum near Brunswick in 1701 and in Düsseldorf in 1714. Picture galleries did not center around individual works of art or art-historical lines of development, but rather around the overall spatial impression conveyed by the venue and the well-being and pleasure of the recipient. Mostly narrow and high, galleries were conceived as indoor gardens, as it were, for taking a pleasant stroll. The paintings and sculptures that lined the walls, often arranged in three or four rows one above the other or mounted in ornate frames, offered a spectrum of inspiring views and stories, sometimes beautiful, sometimes frightening.

Naturally, these galleries were intended to represent the respective princes' splendor and connoisseurship. However, they were visited by a variety of com-

pletely different groups: not only travelers on their "Grand Tour", interested in viewing famous collections, and artists who came wanting to copy individual works, but also the "lower classes". In 1786, for example, a visitor wrote of the Viennese Imperial and Royal Picture Gallery: "On Mondays there is usually a bustling crowd. A good deal of people from the lower classes, craftsmen taking a 'blue Monday', even lowly maids with children in their arms visit the picture gallery for a pleasant afternoon."

These former qualities of the picture gallery also have been revived in many newer museums. In place of the nineteenth-century atmosphere of a consecrated temple or bourgeois teaching institution, they encourage pleasurable strolling through rooms. The Solomon R. Guggenheim Museum, opened in 1959, set an impressive stage for the act of walking with a 432-meter spiral ramp. Likewise specially designed with pedestrians in mind was the Neue Staatsgalerie in Stuttgart (in operation since 1984), through which there runs a public crossing offering picturesque views into the gallery. At the Fundação de Serralves in Porto (1999), the museum was merged with the surrounding park to create an immersive walking and viewing experience. The MAXXI, Museo nazionale delle arti del XXI secolo building in Rome (2010), on the other hand, is intersected by countless ramps, terraces, and free-floating staircases from where one can gaze at one's surroundings. Rising floors, panoramic windows, and winding pathways transform a (mere) visit into a stroll through a "landscape".

This reorientation towards the visitor, however, is also reflected in the new standard of spatial programming: no museum building is conceivable today without a centrally located museum shop, an appealing museum café and/or restaurant, generously sized ticket and information counters, cloakrooms and restrooms, studios for workshops, auditoriums for

← Museum Insel Hombroich: Exhibition Pavilion in the landscape garden.
Building design: Erwin Heerich

lectures, and foyers for receptions. Not all of these rooms may have much to do with a museum's official business (collecting, preserving, researching, exhibiting)—that is, with classic "exhibits"—but they have a lot to do with the people who want to visit it. One could even make the claim that people, when inside the museum with their diverse physical and social requirements, rise to become co-equal exhibits, so to speak. For there is yet another aspect in which the works of art exhibited in the White Cube and their silent visitors resemble each other: in the convention of their simultaneous multifaceted presence and mute isolation, both equally perform a ritual of separation. As the art historian Dorothea von Hantelmann has argued, offering this opportunity to experience emancipation and one's own invention as a subject is in fact one of the central functions of a modern art museum today.

The cultural districts emerging around the world have adopted many of the spatial templates described above, yet they offer a striking counterprogram to the rituals of the interior spaces. It is not only the scenery of their heterogenous buildings that speaks ostentatiously of "ensemble", rather than of "solitude" or "isolation". In their outdoor spaces, people sit or stand together in large numbers. Polyphony thus characterizes not only the spectrum of the assembled cultural providers, but also the ambient noise. In some places, this chorus of voices and sounds feels cozy, as in Gorky Park in Moscow; in others, such as the Southbank Centre in London, it is lively and loud. As a rule, the result is an astonishingly harmonious atmosphere of democratic togetherness, a kind of "culture for all", in which every voice counts equally.

Further reading

Werner Arndt/Werner Bialluch, "Kulturforum. Konzept zur Weiterentwicklung. Senatsbeschluss 16. März 2004 und Informationen zu Geschichte, Planung und Konzeption." Published by Senatsverwaltung für Stadtentwicklung, Berlin 2004. Available online at http://www.stadtentwicklung.berlin.de/planen/staedtebauprojekte/kulturforum/downloads/broschuere_weiterentw_kulturf_040614.pdf (last accessed November 2, 2020).

Matthias Boeckl, "Kulturelle Urbanisierung: Zur Planungsphilosophie von Ortner & Ortner", in: Matthias Boeckl (ed.), MuseumsQuartier Wien. Die Architektur, Vienna 2001, pp. 41–45.

Geneviève Bresc-Bautier, "Le Louvre, une histoire de palais", Paris 1995.

Dorothea von Hantelmann, "How to Do Things with Art. Bedeutsamkeit der Performativität von Kunst", Zurich 2007.

Hilmar Hoffmann, "Das Frankfurter Museumsufer", Frankfurt am Main 2009.

Ekkehard Mai/Eva Hartmann (ed.), "Die Zukunft der Alten Meister. Perspektiven und Konzepte für das Kunstmuseum von heute", Cologne/Weimar/Vienna 2001.

Marion von Osten, "Producing Publics—Making Worlds! Zum Verhältnis von Kunstöffentlichkeit und Gegenöffentlichkeit", in: Gerald Raunig/Ulf Wuggenig (ed.), Publicum. Theorien der Öffentlichkeit, Vienna 2005, pp. 124–139.

Franziska Puhan-Schulz, "Museen und Stadtimagebildung. Amsterdam—Frankfurt/Main—Prag. Ein Vergleich", Bielefeld 2005.

Bénédicte Savoy (ed.), "Tempel der Kunst. Die Entstehung des öffentlichen Museums in Deutschland 1701–1815", Mainz 2006.

Maria Welzig/Anna Stuhlpfarrer (ed.), "Kulturquartiere in ehemaligen Residenzen. Zwischen imperialer Kulisse und urbaner Neubesetzung", Cologne/Weimar/Vienna 2014.

Martin Wentz (ed.), "Die kompakte Stadt" (Die Zukunft des Städtischen. Frankfurter Beiträge, vol. 11), Frankfurt am Main/New York 2000.

Bernd Wiese, "Museums-Ensembles und Städtebau in Deutschland—1815 bis in die Gegenwart. Akteure—Standorte—Stadtgestalt.", St. Augustin 2008.

Quartier des Spectacles

Culture as the Key Factor for Urban Development

by Erwin Uhrmann

The Quartier des Spectacles is part of downtown Montréal, with a growing density of cultural institutions and a network of public squares used mainly for artistic and cultural purposes. The district is freely accessible around the clock. It is home to more than eighty cultural institutions and forty festivals, as well as ongoing cultural programs.

Location	Canada, Montréal (Quebec), Quartier des Spectacles Partnership, 1435, Saint-Alexandre Street, Suite 500, H3A 2G4/city center
Opened	creation of the Quartier des Spectacles Partnership in 2003
Total area	approx. 1 km^2
Number of cultural facilities	approx. 69
Leisure facilities & activities	cafés/restaurants, residential units, shops, etc.
Visitors/year	n/a, due to being an urban district
Architecture	Daoust Lestage (urban design of the Place des Festivals)
Website	quartierdesspectacles.com

History

The Quartier des Spectacles is the urban and cultural center of Montréal. This area was declared a cultural district only relatively recently, in the early 2000s. The existing concentration of cultural institutions, especially those in the performing arts, formed the basis for the decision to push culture as a key factor in the city's future development.

The history of the district stretches back to the nineteenth century, when Montréal was the largest city in the then-state of Canada. Due to its position as a railway hub and port and hence as an economic and cultural center, the city experienced a golden age of expansion, rapid industrialization, and a population boom thanks to several waves of immigration. Several educational institutions settled in the city center. The Collège Sainte-Marie, founded by the Jesuits in 1865, also contained the area's first cultural institution, "l'amphithéâtre du Gesù". In 1914, the Bibliothèque Saint-Sulpice was built. It was the first French-language library in Canada, which had gained independence (from Britain) in 1867.

↑ Place des Festivals
Photo © Stephan Poulin

↖ Previous double page: "Un coeur nomade", Promenade des Artistes
Curator and creative director: Félix Dagenais
Graphic and scenic design: Judith Portier Inc.
Music and sound design: Javier Asencio
Photo © Olivier Gariépy

Canada's first professional francophone theatre, the Gayety Theatre, was founded in 1912. The Cinéma Imperial, with seats for 2,300 people, was built one year later. Over the following decades the district became a center for cabaret. During the prohibition era in the United States between 1920 and 1933, Montréal became a popular tourist destination. Organized crime, prostitution, and illegal gambling flourished equally, and the center soon became the city's red-light district.

Salle Wilfrid-Pelletier, Place des Arts
Photo © Olivier Gariépy

At the end of the 1950s, then-mayor Jean Drapeau, an opera aficionado, initiated the construction of Place des Arts, a cultural area that aimed to enhance the inner city with cultural focal points. The first construction phase was completed in 1963 with the Salle Wilfrid-Pelletier, a multi-functional venue that was to become the home of l'Orchestre symphonique de Montréal, and later, Les Grands Ballets Canadiens and l'Opéra de Montréal.

The 1960s heralded a profound change in the province of Quebec, termed the "Quiet Revolution", manifest in a series of reforms. The secularization of health and education and a series of political and infrastructural measures transformed the province into a welfare state. Canada's centenary celebrations reached a climax with the 1967

Montréal Expo. The city experienced a cultural boom in the following decades, reflected in the founding of several cultural and educational institutions, beginning with the Université du Québec à Montréal (UQAM) campus. The Cinemathèque québécoise, Festival international de Jazz de Montréal, and a range of other festivals drove further cultural developments. In the 1970s, commercial development was also given a boost with the construction of the Complexe Desjardins (1976), a complex consisting of a hotel, a shopping center, and offices. In 1972, the Théâtre du Nouveau Monde (TNM) bought the building at the corner of Ste-Catherine Street and St-Urbain Street, where the Gayety Theatre once performed. Later in 1997, the theater was entirely renovated by architect Dan Hanganu, at the request of Lorraine Pintal, the general and artistic director.

In the 1990s the Musée d'art contemporain was built beside Place des Arts. The idea of the Quartier des Spectacles arose after the addition of the Pierre-Mercure Performance Venue, the Société des arts technologiques, and other institutions: "The task at hand was not to create a neighbourhood from scratch, but rather to identify it, highlight its rich cultural assets and equip it with the infrastructure to accommodate outdoor events."[1] In 2003 the Quartier des Spectacles Partnership was established, comprising an initial twenty members who worked out a vision for the district's further development. Besides a common visual identity, the motto "Live, Learn, Create and Entertain Downtown" was defined as a key factor. In 2007 the City of Montréal and the provincial and federal governments gave the Quartier des Spectacles the green light to develop the Place des Festivals, at the center of the district, near Place des Arts. The building complex, which is connected to Montréal's subway network, now houses six music and theater stages (Maison symphonique, Salle Wilfrid-Pelletier, Théâtre Maisonneuve, Théâtre Jean-Duceppe, Studio-théâtre, Cinquième salle). It is a gathering place in the city and a venue for festivals and for art projects in the public space.

In 2009 the Quartier des Spectacles gained Place des Festivals, a new central square for up to 25,000 people. The square has served ever since as the city's most important venue for festivals, such as the Festival international de Jazz de Montréal.

The Promenade des Artistes was created in the area between the Complexe des sciences Pierre-Dansereau, the campus of Université du Québec à Montréal, and Place des Arts. Eleven glass display cases lining the promenade provide space for temporary art installations. The promenade also connects Place des Arts with Le Parterre, a 3,500 m^2 square with grass lawns. In addition to the public spaces, new government and privately financed culturally focused institutions have been set up, including 2-22 and the Maison symphonique de Montréal. In addition to residential buildings and creative businesses, new cultural buildings have emerged recently, such as the National Film Board of Canada and the Wilder Espace Danse, home of Les Grands Ballets.

Its open urban structure and progressive development mean that the Quartier des Spectacles is in a state of continual change.

Architecture

The Quartier des Spectacles is an urban area that has developed organically. This is reflected in the wide variety of architectural periods, styles, and urban development initiatives. The Bibliothèque Saint-Sulpice, built between 1912 and 1914, is an example of Beaux Arts architecture in Quebec.

Place des Arts, located in the heart of the Quartier des Spectacles, was planned in the 1950s by the architectural partnership of Affleck, Desbarats, Dimakopoulos, Lebensold, Michaud & Sise to be a cultural district with several facilities and a public square. Six buildings for the performing arts were built in the first phase, completed in 1963. The most recent addition, completed in 2011, is the Maison symphonique, designed by Diamond Schmitt Architects.

The Musée d'art contemporain de Montréal, completed in 1992, was designed by architects Jodoin Lamarre Pratte & Associés. In 2017, in order to double its exhibition spaces, and also to better integrate the building into its environment, an architecture competition for the design of a conversion and extension was launched. The design by Saucier+Perrotte Architectes/GLCRM & Associés Architectes was selected by a consortium of Quebec architects in 2018.

A process of urban development based around cultural use has been in progress in the district, especially since the Quartier des Spectacles Partnership was established. This has led to the restructuring of its more than 300,000 m² of public space, based on integrated planning.

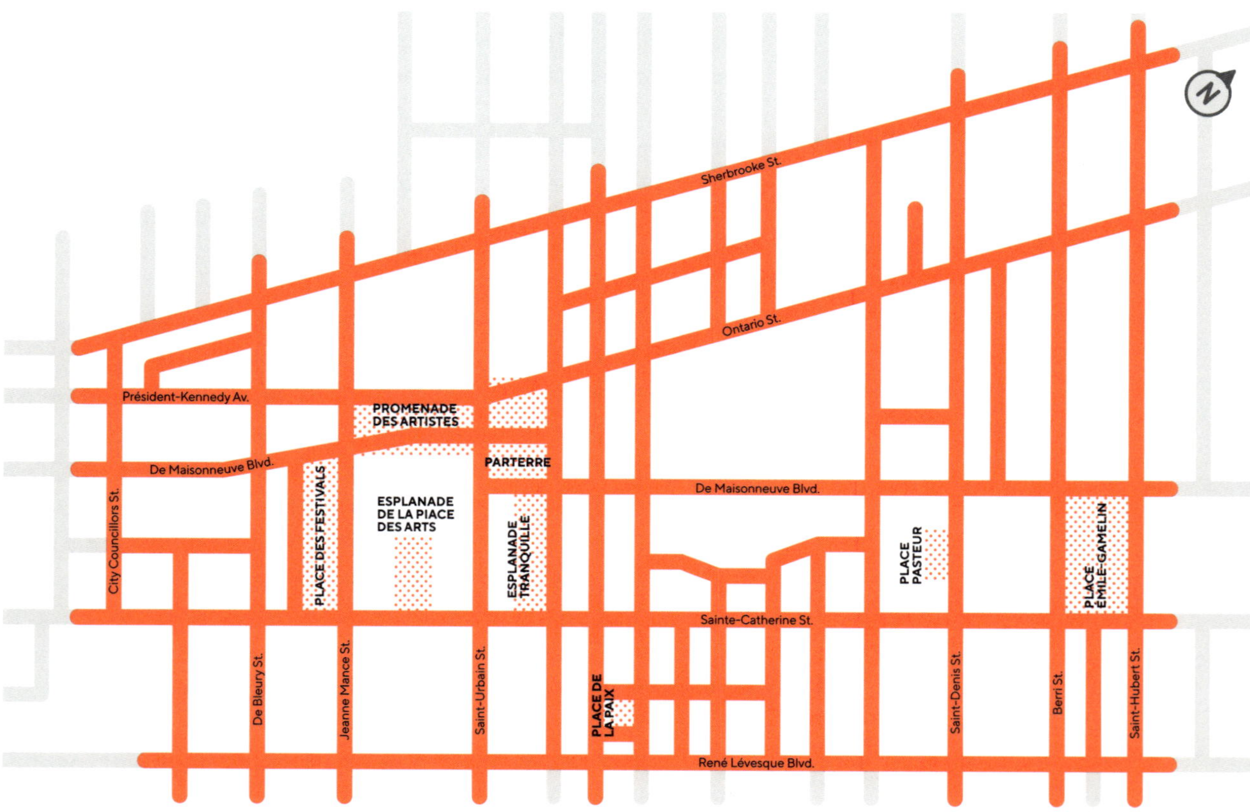

← The National Film Board of Canada
Photo © Olivier Gariépy

→ "EN FORME!"—Video projection by Champagne Club Sandwich, Président Kennedy Pavillon, UQAM
Photo © Martine Doyon

In 2009, architects Daoust Lestage designed the 14,400 m² Place des Festivals from both a landscape and urban planning perspective. The square is both a resting spot with an interactive fountain and a public space for numerous festivals.

The six-story multifunctional building 2-22 by Ædifica and Giles Huot Architectes opened in 2012. It functions as a landmark of contemporary architecture within the district's overall ensemble. The recessed, angled entrance area and double façade made of wood on the inside and glass on the outside open the building up to passersby.

Organization

The art and cultural institutions within the Quartier des Spectacles are independent of one another, both financially and in terms of their programming. Common focal points, activities, and the further development of the district are coordinated within the Quartier des Spectacles Partnership.

The Partnership operates as a non-profit organization comprising eighty-five active institutions and businesses. A team attends to the day-to-day operations and reports to a Board of Directors, which is made up of representatives from the existing sectors such as culture, business, and education, as well as from the City of Montréal and local residents. The Board of Directors decides on the basic development of the area. The Partnership coordinates the district's various players and its external networking. It is responsible for the joint cultural programs and the management of the district's eight public squares. The artistic

Urban terrace Prenez-place!
Jean-François St-Onge and Marie-Andrée Groleau, ADHOC Architects
Dance performance "Manon fait de la danse–Snow White"
Photo © Eva Blue

focus is on participatory installations, urban design, animation, video projections, and exhibitions. The Partnership is also responsible for the program and district communication.

The City of Montréal provides eighty percent of the district's funding. The remaining twenty percent comes from the institutions in the Partnership. Spaces are not rented out commercially; rather, income is generated through the leasing of the publicly displayed artworks to institutions in other countries.

Structure

The Quartier des Spectacles, located in the district of Ville-Marie, covers an area of 1 km². The district is the cultural heart of Montréal, containing the highest concentration of cultural institutions in North America, with a total capacity of 28,000 seats. It is bordered by Sherbrooke Street to the north, René-Lévesque Boulevard to the south, Saint-Hubert Street to the east, and City Councillors Street to the west. The area is freely accessible around the clock and can be reached by several means of public transport. As part of the city center, the area has residential and office buildings, restaurants, shops, hotels, banks, and various public facilities. The area has 50,000 residents, 45,000 workers, and 50,000 students.

Programming

All in all, the district comprises eighty cultural venues, hosts forty festivals, and has thirty-three performance halls, thirty-four museums, galleries, and art spaces, eight public squares, and seven institutions for art education. More than fifty cultural events take place every day.

One programmatic focus of the cooperation between the institutions at the Quartier des Spectacles is the design and use of public space. This program is oriented towards contemporary discourse and current developments regarding the art in the public spaces. Various types of artistic interventions in the urban space—whether temporary or permanent—are realized. The spectrum of art forms ranges from visual and digital art to the performing arts, but also includes architecture and design.

The project "Luminothérapie", in which interactive light installations are set up every winter in Place des Festivals, serves as an illustration of this strategy. Places are awarded through a competition. In many cases, the works shown are then loaned out to other cultural districts or museums.

The installation "21 Balançoires", created by Daily tous les jours in collaboration with the behavioral scientist Luc-Alain Giraldeau of the Université du Québec à Montréal and composer Radwan Ghazi Moumneh, follows a playful principle. The artwork resembles a swing, and the viewer is invited to use it. Each individual swing generates a note, and a melody is created when swinging for a longer period of time.

In addition to permanent projects, numerous events are held in the district's various squares. One example is Les Jardins Gamelin, which features a large green area and offers a broad range of content and programs, ranging from music, circus, and dance to outdoor art.

← Les Jardins Gamelin, Place Émilie-Gamelin
Photo © Bruno Destombes

→ "21 Balançoires", by Daily tous les jours
Promenade des Artistes
Photo © Ulysse Lemerise/OSA

Impact

With the Quartier des Spectacles Partnership, culture was defined as a central factor for Montréal's development. With the largest concentration of cultural players in North America, the district radiates a strong international appeal.

After an initial mission that focused strongly on urban restructuring, the Quartier des Spectacles Partnership concentrated on content-related synergies and matters of programming from 2009 onward, following the opening of Place des Festivals. In addition to the existing offerings, the Partnership is focused on promoting the performing arts, creating a cultural program, enlivening the public spaces, generating artistic stimuli, and promoting the district as a tourist destination in the heart of Montréal.

Bringing art in all its diverse forms into the public spaces has become an essential factor in revitalizing the public squares. The Quartier des Spectacles Partnership developed a strategy of loaning out works that were created specifically for outdoor public spaces to international institutions. By focusing on installations and interactive digital art, the district actively networks with other museums and cultural districts throughout the world and promotes artists by providing an international platform for their work. This strategy meant that twelve works could be shown in forty-seven cities throughout the world between 2016 and 2020.

↖ LOOP
Designers: Olivier Girouard, Jonathan Villeneuve and Ottoblix, Place des Festivals
Photo © Ulysse Lemerise/OSA

↑ Oscillation, by Ryan Swanson, The Urban Conga, Quartier Latin
Photo © Eva Blue

→ "Dans ma cour … ç'a du chien!", conception by Mélanie Crespin, Sainte-Catherine Street
Photo © Vincent Sauriol-Nadeau - Shoot Studio

1 https://www.quartierdesspectacles.com/en/about/history-and-vision/ (last accessed April 16, 2021)

Southbank Centre

From Festival Hall to Cultural District

by Irene Preißler

Situated on the banks of the Thames the Southbank Centre's site is home to multiple venues, orchestras, bars, restaurants and street food markets, making it the UK's largest arts center and one of London's most popular meeting places. In addition to its program of cultural events, the Centre offers opportunities for relaxation.

Location	United Kingdom, London, Belvedere Road/ city center
Opened	1951
Total area	45,000 m² (11 acres)
Number of cultural facilities	4
Leisure facilities & activities	public open spaces, cafés and restaurants
Visitors/year	4 million
Architecture	Sir Robert Matthew, Sir Leslie Martin, Allies and Morrison, Higgs and Hill, Hubert Bennett, Jack Whittle, F. G. West, Geoffrey Horsfall, Feilden Clegg Bradley Studios (FCBStudios)
Website	www.southbankcentre.co.uk

History and Architecture

The history of the Southbank Centre began with the construction of the Royal Festival Hall, one of the Centre's four cultural facilities today. It was built as part of the Festival of Britain, which was intended to restore morale following the Second World War. The first designs were drawn up as early as 1948. In addition to pavilions for the festival, the principal element was to be the construction of a new concert hall for London to replace the Queen's Hall, which had been destroyed in a bombing raid in 1941. Construction of the Royal Festival Hall, designed by Sir Robert Matthew and Sir Leslie Martin, commenced in 1949. Large, open foyers with bars and restaurants were to create a meeting place for all, rather than a venue intended only for an elite public. The main material used was concrete—the favored material of modernism—in combination with luxurious elements such as wood and limestone, to create a brilliant white exterior that would stand out against the dark gray of the city. On May 3, 1951, after a construction period of only eighteen months, the new 2,700-seat concert hall was opened in the presence of King George VI and Queen Elizabeth II.

In 1965, following an eight-month renovation, the Royal Festival Hall re-opened with a new ticket office, larger backstage areas, offices, and a new riverside entrance. Two new concert halls designed by Higgs and Hill, the Queen Elizabeth Hall and the Purcell Room, were added in 1967. The Queen Elizabeth Hall is a typical example of Brutalism with

↑ Royal Festival Hall Building
Photo © India Roper-Evans

↖ Previous double page:
The Hayward Gallery Building
Photo © Morley Von Sternberg

minimal ornamental elements. Together with the Royal Festival Hall, the three halls became known as the South Bank Concert Halls. The opening of the Hayward art gallery (later Hayward Gallery) followed in 1968. All three buildings were conceived as extensions of the Southbank Centre by Hubert Bennett in collaboration with Jack Whittle, F. G. West, and Geoffrey Horsfall.

An "open foyer" policy was adopted in 1983 to provide visitors with easy access. The Royal Festival Hall's foyers would be open to the public seven days a week, around the clock, and for free, with exhibitions, jazz performances, afternoon concerts, and much more.

In 1988 the Southbank Centre, comprising the Royal Festival Hall, the Hayward Gallery, Queen Elizabeth Hall, and Purcell Room, became an independent cultural institution. In the same year, the Poetry Library moved into the Royal Festival Hall.

Renovation of the Royal Festival Hall began in 1994 under the direction of Allies and Morrison architects. An international competition for the redesign of all the buildings was won by the Richard Rogers Partnership. The project was to be financed through the National Lottery Fund; however, the costs proved too high, and the project was never realized.

→ The Hayward Gallery, inside
Photo © Morley Von Sternberg

↓ Queen Elizabeth Hall
Photo © Pete Woodhead

Queen Elizabeth Hall Foyer
Photo © Garry Jones/Victor Frankowski

The Southbank Centre established a new corporate identity in 1995. Devised by CDT Design, it was based primarily on the Royal Festival Hall and Hayward Gallery as key elements. The previous name of South Bank Centre was abbreviated to SBC.

In 2018 the Queen Elizabeth Hall reopened following a three-year renovation. The redesign by Feilden Clegg Bradley Studios (FCBStudios) concentrated on the renovation of the auditorium, foyer, and backstage area. The entrance area was revamped and new ventilation, lighting, and production equipment installed to offer visitors an even better artistic experience.

Thousands of artists have performed at the Southbank Centre over the years, including Brian Wilson, Grace Jones, Daniel Barenboim, Alfred Brendel, the Alban Berg Quartet, and Gustavo Dudamel. The Centre has also hosted a large number of events and festivals, such as the WOW—Women of the World Festival in 2010, which today is one of the largest women's festivals in the world; the Festival of the World in 2012 to mark the Olympic Games; the Festival of Love in 2014 which invited seventy bridal couples to say "I do" on the Royal Festival Hall stage; and an interactive exhibition in 2016 to mark the 100th birthday of children's author Roald Dahl.

Organization

Until 1985, the Royal Festival Hall and the future Southbank Centre —with the exception of the Hayward Gallery—were under the direction of London County Council (later Greater London Council). Hayward (later Hayward Gallery) was under the direct control of the Arts Council from 1968 to 1985. After the dissolution of Greater London Council in 1985, the Arts Council took over direction of the entire Southbank Centre. The South Bank Board was founded at the same time and, as part of the Arts Council, eventually took over management of all three concert halls.

The Southbank Centre, comprising the Royal Festival Hall, Hayward Gallery, Queen Elizabeth Hall, and Purcell Room, has been an independent cultural institution since 1988. It is led by a chief executive, who reports to the Board of Governors.

Funding is provided largely by the Arts Council. Additional income is generated by ticket and shop sales, donations, and sponsoring.

← National Poetry Library
Photo © Pete Woodhead

→ The Royal Festival Hall
Photo © LIA VITTONE PHOTOGRAPHY, Lia Vittone

Structure

The Southbank Centre is part of London's South Bank district, which stretches from Lambeth Bridge to McLaren House and Blackfriars Bridge. In the midst of London's cultural quarter, it extends directly along the Thames from the Golden Jubilee Bridge to Waterloo Bridge, bordered by the Queen's Walk. The area is freely accessible around the clock and can be reached by all forms of public transport. The various cultural institutions have different opening hours.

The Royal Festival Hall
Photo © India Roper-Evans

Programming

Following the principle that art and creativity can change everyone's life, help to overcome differences, and bring society closer together, the Southbank Centre aims not only to offer cultural experiences and present art, but also to inspire culture itself and give artists the opportunity to create the extraordinary.

At the same time, it strives to provide something for everyone: "Not everyone will love everything, but we make sure there's something for everyone."[1] The Southbank Centre sees itself as a place that everyone can identify with, and where they feel respected and appreciated.

A comprehensive outreach program is aimed at schools, organizations, and private individuals. In addition to events, workshops, and festivals, many free of charge, there are opportunities to work with established artists from a diverse range of fields.

The Southbank Centre comprises four cultural institutions in total: the Royal Festival Hall, the Hayward Gallery, the Queen Elizabeth Hall, and the Purcell Room.

The 2,700-seat Royal Festival Hall is one of London's leading concert venues. It is also the home of the Clore Ballroom, used for dance workshops, the free-to-use National Poetry Library, the Archive Studio, which contains information on the history of the Centre and past events, the Southbank Centre Shop, the Riverside Terrace Cafe, the Central Bar, and the Skylon Restaurant. The Queen Elizabeth Hall and the Purcell Room provide two additional event locations for concerts, performances, and talks. The Purcell Room's 295 seats provide an intimate setting for readings, screenings, discussions, and smaller events. The Hayward Gallery shows contemporary art in a changing program of exhibitions.

The Southbank Centre is also home to eight orchestras, of which four are resident orchestras (the London Philharmonic Orchestra, the Philharmonia Orchestra, the Orchestra of the Age of Enlightenment, and the London Sinfonietta) and four are partner orchestras (the Aurora Orchestra, the BBC Concert Orchestra, Chineke!, and the National Youth Orchestra).

In addition to the concerts, performances, events, and exhibitions held in the various venues, a variety of cultural events are held in the outdoor areas, such as Winter Light, in which fifteen artistic works were displayed throughout the entire site and along the bank from November 2020 to February 2021. The exhibition was created specially for the winter months and exhibited artworks that have taken inspiration from light, color, and the poetics of space.

Royal Festival Hall Auditorium
Photo © Victor Frankowski

Impact

With around 4.5 million visitors every year, the Southbank Centre is one of the five most visited tourist attractions in Great Britain. Twenty percent of visitors come from Great Britain, and forty-five percent come from overseas,[2] making the Southbank Centre a major contributor to international tourism.

The Southbank Centre is also a creator of jobs and high indirect profitability: in addition to the 456 people directly employed by Southbank Centre, approximately 900 suppliers from all over the UK provide construction, security, or creative services.[3] In numbers, the Southbank Centre expends approximately twenty-five million pounds per year on staff and service providers, fifteen million of which goes to businesses operating in London.[4] This contributes substantially toward strengthening the economy. Additionally, companies can hire workspace on the site temporarily or during festivals: in addition to the external cafés and restaurants, the Southbank Centre has thirty-six premises for shops and eleven for pop-ups, attracting visitors with an affinity for business, as well as those with an interest in culture.

M.I.A. performing at Meltdown Festival
Photo © Mike Massaro

← Southbank Centre Food Market

→ The Royal Festival Hall/Members Bar

Photos © India Roper-Evans

At the same time, the Southbank Centre helps to reduce social disadvantage through its extensive outreach program for schools. As part of a partnership with schools in the boroughs of Lambeth and Southwark, children, especially those from low-income households, are brought closer to art and culture in order to overcome social divisions. One example is the Imagine Children's Festival 2019, part of the Imagine a Story project. Teachers and their pupils were asked to continue a story by children's author Joseph Coelho. All participants were then invited to London to meet one another and hear the finished story. The project encouraged children and teachers to engage in creative writing.

The foundation of the Southbank Centre began with the idea of using art and culture to raise society's morale in difficult times and thus contribute to general well-being. To this day, the Southbank Centre remains engaged in actions and initiatives for the benefit of people. During the coronavirus pandemic, for example, SBC initiated Art by Post, a project in which small parcels containing poetry and visual art were sent free of charge to people living alone. Other initiatives include Streetwise Opera, a project that uses singing to empower people recovering from homelessness, and "Southbank Centre's free afternoon tea dancers" and the (B)old Festival, both aimed at bringing visitors—especially older ones—out of social isolation.

The Southbank Centre thus not only plays a central role in the economic development of the entire South Bank area, but, as the cultural center of the city, also contributes significantly to London's quality of life.

1 https://www.southbankcentre.co.uk/about/mission-values (last accessed April 4, 2021).

2 Hatch Regeneris, Economic and Social Impact Assessment of The Southbank Centre. A Final Report by Hatch, August 2020, p. ii, available at: https://bynder.southbankcentre.co.uk/m/1dd385297747 1c14/original/Southbank-Centre_Economic-and-Social-Impact-Report_Nov-2020.pdf (last accessed April 4, 2021).

3 Ibid.

4 Ibid.

The Arts Centre Te Matatiki Toi Ora

From Campus of Education to Place of Culture and Leisure

by Irene Preißler

“Te Matatiki Toi Ora” means “spring of well-being or living art” in the Māori language of Aotearoa New Zealand. This Māori term has become something of a leitmotif for The Arts Centre in Ōtautahi Christchurch. Situated in the heart of the city, its various buildings form Christchurch’s largest cohesive collection of historic architecture, featuring a wide variety of arts and creative organizations. Visitors can also stroll and relax in the inner quadrangles. There are shops as well as cafés, restaurants, and cinemas. The Centre’s ongoing offer includes cultural events, exhibitions, performances, workshops, and educational programs. The focus is on arts, culture, heritage, recreation, and well-being.

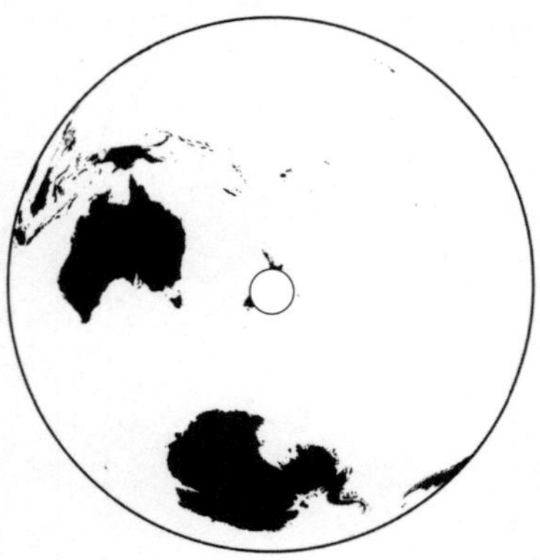

Location	New Zealand, Ōtautahi Christchurch, 2 Worcester Boulevard/city center
Opened	1978
Total area	approx. 22,000 m²
Number of cultural institutions	6
Leisure facilities & activities	public open spaces, cafés/restaurants, market, cinemas, creative endeavors, and public events
Visitors/year	650,000
Architecture	Benjamin Woolfield Mountfort, Samuel Hurst Seager, Thomas Cane, William Armson, Cyril Mountfort, Collins & Harman, Francis William Petre
Website	www.artscentre.org.nz

History and Architecture

The history of The Arts Centre stretches back to pre-colonial times. The land was originally used by Māori. There were no permanent settlements, but larger sites where people lived for certain periods of time.

The land was purchased in 1873 for the construction of Canterbury College, now Te Whare Wānanga o Waitaha The University of Canterbury. Benjamin Woolfield Mountfort designed some of the initial buildings, including the Clock Tower and Great Hall, and as one of New Zealand's best-known architects of the colonial era, his Victorian Gothic Revival buildings continue to dominate the cityscape of Ōtautahi Christchurch today. The first building to be completed was the Clock Tower in 1877, which houses the interactive museum Rutherford's Den, named after the Nobel Prize-winning physicist (and Canterbury College alumnus), Ernest, Lord Rutherford, who studied here for a time.

In 1878, The Christchurch Girls' High School moved on site; designed by architect Thomas Cane this later became the School of Art. The Christchurch Boys' High School followed in 1881. The Great Hall, used for ceremonies and lectures as well as musical and dance performances and festivals, was added in 1882. Today, the Hall, which offers free admission to visitors, is best known for its enormous 4,000-piece stained-glass window by Martin Travers. It was completed in 1938, twenty years after Travers produced his design.

↖ Previous double page:
South Quadrangle, February 2020, artwork: Seung Yul Oh, Conduct Cumulus, 2017. Produced by SCAPE Public Art.

↓ Great Hall, June 2016

Photos © Johannes van Kan

Numerous other buildings were built in the following years to accommodate the university's continuous expansion. These included Canterbury College's School of Engineering, the Biology and Observatory buildings, the Gymnasium for the Boys' High School, a theater and event room, the Chemistry and Physics buildings, and the Library, which was planned by Samuel Hurst Seager as the center between two inner quadrangles.

The university gradually relocated out of the site between the 1950s and 1970s. Over the years many notable personalities studied there, including women's rights activist Ada Wells; the first female accepted to study at Canterbury College and the first female honors graduate (Master of Arts) in the British Empire, Helen Connon; Nobel Prize-winning physicist, Ernest, Lord Rutherford; the first Māori graduate, Sir Āpirana Ngata; champion of women's right to education, Alice Candy; Rita Angus, one of the most important New Zealand artists of the twentieth century; the philosopher Sir Karl Raimund Popper; and famed New Zealand children's author Dame Margaret Mahy.

In 1978, The Arts Centre of Christchurch Trust formally took over operation of the area from The Arts Centre of Christchurch Inc. The Arts Centre Market has been one of the area's main attractions since 1981. Featuring local products and arts and crafts, it remains one of Ōtautahi Christchurch's most popular markets, with themed markets throughout the year.

The Arts Centre complex of 23 buildings has been listed as a Category 1 heritage site by Heritage New Zealand Pouhere Taonga since 1990.

The Arts Centre Te Matatiki Toi Ora from the corner of Rolleston Avenue and Hereford Street, January 2019
Photo © Johannes van Kan

Major earthquakes struck the region on September 4, 2010 and February 22, 2011. Twenty-two of the Centre's twenty-three buildings were severely damaged and, in some cases, destroyed. By 2021, as part of an extensive restoration program, around two thirds of the site had been rebuilt and made accessible. For the restoration of the Great Hall and Clock Tower, The Arts Centre was awarded the Award of Merit at the UNESCO Asia-Pacific Awards for Cultural Heritage Conservation.

Currently, The Arts Centre is restoring the Observatory Tower, which will once again house the Townsend Teece Telescope, and the Biology and Physics buildings, which will become a boutique hotel and are due to open in mid-2022.

The Gym, July 2014
Photo © Johannes van Kan

Structure

Situated in the center of Ōtautahi Christchurch, The Arts Centre spans an entire city block, framed by Worcester Boulevard, Rolleston Avenue, Hereford and Montreal Streets. Most buildings date from the twentieth century. The spatial concept of the west side developed during the construction of the Library in 1916, following the plans of architect Samuel Hurst Seager. It comprises two square inner courtyards enclosed by cloisters. The east side is more open toward the street and dominated by two newer buildings: the former Student Union building, closed since the earthquakes, and the Registry Additions building, which today houses the organizations SCAPE Public Art, The Physics Room offices and contemporary art gallery, Frank Film, and a café.

Organization

In 1978, following the departure of Canterbury University, The Arts Centre was established as a charitable trust and designated by the New Zealand parliament in 2015 as a "cultural asset of local, national, and international heritage significance"[1] of New Zealand. This was accompanied by the passing of The Arts Centre of Christchurch Trust Act, which lays down the objectives of the trust. The trust is governed by an independent board. The board's role is to ensure The Arts Centre performs its duty of promoting and developing the arts, culture, the creative industries, and education.

The Arts Centre's Director is responsible for the site's management, supported by the Finance and Administration Manager, Operations Manager, and Creative Director.

Programming

Under the motto "restoring memories and creating futures",[2] The Arts Centre's vision rests on three pillars: the continual development of the Centre while safeguarding its historical importance; the strengthening of interest in arts, culture, creativity, and education; and a lively exchange with the public through an integrative program.

Thanks to The Arts Centre's mix of cultural and educational spaces, shops, restaurants, offices, and publicly accessible open spaces, visitors of all kinds encounter one another here. Some are there to visit an art gallery or exhibition, drop in and hear some live music, while others seek relaxation or come for the architecture. A key element, therefore, is exchange with and involvement of the public.

Just as diverse as its public are the Centre's various facilities. They include the community exhibition space Pūmanawa; Rutherford's Den, a multifunctional experience named after the Nobel Prize-winning physicist Ernest, Lord Rutherford, where science, history, and discovery come to life; the Teece Museum of Classical Antiquities,

← Rutherford's Den Lecture Theatre, May 2019

→ Classics Boardroom, March 2018

Photos © Johannes van Kan

which houses historical artefacts; The Physics Room, a working space available to emerging artists; and The Central Art Gallery, which showcases the works of well-known contemporary New Zealand artists.

The Arts Centre is also home to Canterbury Academy of Dance, where promising young dancers receive training, and Lumière Cinemas, whose two vintage-style movie theaters offer arthouse cinematic experiences. Also on site are Paint & Sip Studio, Aotearoa New Zealand's first social painting destination, and Fragranzi, an artisan perfume studio where you can create your own fragrance.

SCAPE Public Art, an initiative also based at The Arts Centre, has been presenting works of art in public spaces throughout the year since 1996. Now one of the leading contemporary arts organizations in New Zealand, SCAPE has made a substantial contribution to the image and appeal of Ōtautahi Christchurch by displaying works by both local and international artists throughout the city. Within The Arts Centre, SCAPE has exhibited works by artists including Cat Auburn, Audrey Baldwin, Holly Best, Piri Cowie, Antony Gormley, Sam Harrison, Gregor Kregar, Nina Oberg Humphries, Seung Yul Oh, George Rickey, Kazu Nakagawa, and Greer Twiss.

Performative works and large-scale installations are also realized in the annual Arts Centre Sculpture Festival. One sculpture from Antony Gormley's two-part work "STAY", from the "SCAPE 8 New Intimacies" series of 2015–16, is featured as a permanent installation. The other sculpture is positioned in the Ōtākaro Avon River.

← Lumière Cinemas, February 2020

→ Bunsen Cafè, March 2017

Photos © Johannes van Kan

At Rekindle, workshops teach the responsible handling of renewable resources, while Arts Centre Education offers various educational programs and workshops. Meanwhile, the University of Canterbury Classics and Music department at The Arts Centre hosts undergraduate and postgraduate courses, lectures, concerts, and much more.

In addition, the Creative Residency programme gives artists and creatives the opportunity to live and work on site. The four double rooms available can be rented out to visitors when not occupied by resident artists.

With its Creative Residency programme and facilities such as The Physics Room, The Arts Centre offers artists the opportunity to live and work on site and provides them with spaces for putting on events, whereby international exchanges can be established.

← World Buskers Festival in the North Quadrangle, January 2017

→ School of Art building Open Day, lutenist Kiel McEntee, March 2019

Photos © Johannes van Kan

Arts Centre Education, April 2021
Photo © Johannes van Kan

Impact

The Arts Centre occupies the so-called Cultural Precinct in the center of Ōtautahi Christchurch. The Canterbury Museum, Christchurch Art Gallery Te Puna o Waiwhetū, and the Centre of Contemporary Art Toi Moroki are also in the immediate vicinity.

Conceived more than 150 years ago as the cultural heart of Canterbury Province, several cultural, educational, governmental, scientific, and religious buildings were built within an area of 1 km^2 along the River Ōtākaro Avon.

In 2014, following the devastating earthquake of 2011, the city approved a rebuilding plan which aims to make the center of Ōtautahi Christchurch "the thriving heart of an international city".[3] The emphasis is on the city's rich cultural and natural heritage. Ōtautahi Christchurch's historical heritage will remain a central element of its identity: new buildings are required to fit harmoniously into the cityscape and interact with the surrounding streets and neighborhood. The planned Performing Arts Precinct due to be opened in late 2023 will also see the creation of a separate neighborhood for the performing arts. Existing cultural institutions such as The Arts Centre are already integrated into the reconstruction.

A 2019 study revealed that the arts play a major role in the lives of Ōtautahi Christchurch's population.[4] Only thirteen percent stated they had not consumed any kind of arts or culture in the previous twelve months. The goal therefore is to continue to appeal to the broad public and give the population the opportunity to consume or actively participate in arts and culture in different ways.

Here, The Arts Centre plays a central role. Firstly, it is a center of and for the arts, for all people of Ōtautahi Christchurch and visitors; and secondly, arts, culture and heritage initiatives are central to the Centre's annual calendar of events.

1 Arts Centre of Christchurch Trust Act 2015, available at https://legislation.govt.nz/act/private/2015/0001/latest/DLM6150206.html (last accessed April 4, 2021).

2 https://www.artscentre.org.nz/about-us/our-vision/ (last accessed March 30, 2021).

3 Christchurch Central Recovery Plan, 2014, p. 27, available at https://ceraarchive.dpmc.govt.nz/documents/christchurch-central-recovery-plan (last accessed April 4, 2021).

4 Christchurch City Council, Life in Christchurch 2018, Arts Culture Heritage. Monitoring and Research, March 2019, available at https://www.ccc.govt.nz/assets/Documents/The-Council/Reporting-Monitoring/LIC2018ArtsCultureHeritageReport-FINAL.pdf (last accessed April 4, 2021).

World Without Scenes: Future Challenges for Cultural Districts

by Gail Lord

Vienna's MuseumsQuartier has created a "cultural scene" which has transformed the city's narrative.
Photo © Hertha Hurnaus

Vienna's MuseumsQuartier reminds us that successful cultural districts are constructed, not born. Cultural districts take time and foresight to develop, as well as inspiration. There was a turbulent fifteen-year gestation period before the implementation of the MuseumsQuartier in 1990—and that was about five years prior to Austria joining the EU and my own modest consulting engagement in this complex scene, which opened in 2001.

I use the term "scene" with intentionality, because the MuseumsQuartier shifted Vienna's narrative from that of the capital of the waltz and imperial symbols to a city of contemporaneity. I am immediately reminded of the Leonard Cohen line "I love the country but I can't stand the scene".[1] Vienna needed to change the "scene" and the MuseumsQuartier cultural district was the means.

The creative scene at the heart of the MuseumsQuartier's seventy cultural facilities is a socially dynamic space where younger residents and visitors can meet freely without having to pay an admission fee or having to buy even a cup of coffee—and this in the city that nurtured the coffee house as a social space. Coffee houses are in themselves "scenes", whether in Mecca, where they are said to have been invented in the fifteenth century, Istanbul in the sixteenth, Vienna in the nineteenth, or New York in the twentieth century, where artists, students, intellectuals, and commerce meet to exchange news and ideas through storytelling, newspapers, and now WiFi. The buzz of a cultural district lies in the interaction between the producers and consumers of ideas. Coffee houses play an important role, as do bars, studios, cultural industries, galleries, and museums—and, most importantly, the spaces between them.

Scenes[2] comes in many shapes, sizes, and themes such as finance (Wall Street), markets (Barcelona's La Rambla), jazz (New Orleans's French District), fine art (Paris's Left Bank), and ideas (London's Knowledge Quarter), to name just the famous ones. Depending on the amenities, authenticities, and multiple meanings, people move in and out of scenes according to their interests and stage of life.

London's "Knowledge Quarter" is an alternative approach to the traditional cultural district. It includes 102 knowledge-based organizations such as museums, research institutes, universities and a major newspaper in the dynamic walkable King's Cross neighborhood.
Photo: The Granary Square, Knowledge Quarter, London, 2020

With seventy museums and cultural institutions, the MuseumsQuartier cultural district attracts both cultural producers and cultural consumers because of its many authentic institutions, from dance to a children's exploration museum and modern art. It also becomes a compelling destination because of the multiple meanings that emerge from the complex texture of the architectural environment that grafts new structures onto the old.

In the MuseumsQuartier, the space between is a porous hangout surrounded by the redesigned and rebuilt eighteenth- and nineteenth-century stables—an immersion in architectural complexity and contradiction,[3] a diversity of human identities, impromptu events, and the means of escape—it is a pedestrian flow-through between distinct city neighborhoods. As a result, for the past decade Vienna has been leading international city rankings[4] not only in tourism, but also in quality of life and innovation.

The MuseumsQuartier is a planned cultural district, but most cultural districts just happen in cities and are dependent on patterns of the real estate market, urban growth, and where museums, theaters, studios, and cultural industries have collocated. Low rents and a growing population of highly educated young people are essential factors in the sustainability of cultural districts. The benefits of cultural districts to both the economy and quality of life of cities include:

- → Co-marketing around a compelling theme;
- → Shared transportation and service infrastructure;
- → Influence on city policies with respect to noise, hours, and security;
- → Urban regeneration;
- → City branding;
- → Efficiency for the tourism industry;
- → Collaboration in event creation;
- → Creating gathering places for social cohesion and the creative economy; and
- → Contributing to city GDP.

What Could Possibly Go Wrong?

The Covid-19 pandemic demonstrates how frail each of these benefits can prove in the face of a major disaster. The pandemic created a world without scenes. It also made us realize that the challenges to our cities and cultural districts already existed before the pandemic. Hopefully, this book is being read during a post-pandemic phase of scene rebuilding. There are five major present and future challenges that require attention for the renewal of cultural districts to ensure their sustainability as vibrant scenes: tourism dependency, balancing production and consumption, climate change, property costs, and governance.

Tourism Dependency

The pandemic demonstrates that over-dependency on tourism undermines cultural districts. When tourism is strong, the numbers mask weaknesses in local and regional engagement. For example, the drastic reduction in attendance at London's national museums below what was anticipated when safety measures were implemented revealed that local visitors pre-pandemic overwhelmingly had been in older age groups, who naturally stayed away for health reasons during the open periods of the pandemic. When tourism accounts for as much as seventy percent of attendance, as is the case for many national museums that anchor cultural districts, changes in travel patterns due to trade wars, armed conflict, financial crises, strikes, and epidemics can reduce the district to a shadow of its former self. Then there is the question of relevance—catering for the global traveler may alienate local and regional residents who yearn for entirely different meanings and diversions.

Balancing Production and Consumption

When cultural districts become too focused on the consumer aspects of culture at the expense of production, they risk becoming stale and homogenized, featuring the same shows and shops as other global destinations. The production of cultural expression is typically assisted by the government through artist grants, operating subsidies, and education funding. The consumer side consists mainly of private expenditures such as ticketing, retail sales, and corporate sponsorship that responds to consumer demand. Governments have successively decreased their arts and museum support over the past forty years, so cultural districts have become lopsided with fewer opportunities for arts production. Incorporating art schools and research institutes in cultural districts, as in London's Knowledge Quarter,[5] has had the beneficial effect of increasing the energy from researchers, artists, and students, who create new ideas and experiences. Seattle has used zoning to protect places where art and crafts such as glass-blowing and artisanal cheese-making are produced, with the aim of balancing production and consumption in some light industrial districts. The presence of artist live-work spaces (when allowed by city zoning) makes cultural districts more lively scenes. The decreasing public sector investment in arts production and the consequent consumerism and privatization occurring in cultural districts poses a challenge to the creativity and authenticity which is the very raison d'etre of cultural districts.

Climate Change

Climate change affects every aspect of life on earth. There is growing action—especially among young people—to control carbon emissions to save our planet. The cultural building boom starting in the 1980s resulted in over-building for the requirements of the twenty-first century, which demands energy reduction, efficient space utilization, and safety measures for future epidemics. The future for culture and education is hybrid—equally online and on-site. So cultural districts must care for outdoor public space as much as if not more than indoor space. In this regard, Vienna's MuseumsQuartier has been exemplary. The collocation of diverse public attractions in districts encourages public transport and reduces car traffic. However, cultural districts will be expected to do more to combat global warming and to lead, even when some of their member organizations are not ready to do so.

Many cultural districts are on waterfronts. Waterfronts are often former industrial lands that have been rehabilitated as cultural and tourism destinations. Rising water levels will threaten the very physical fabric of many waterfront cultural districts, for example in New Orleans, Cape Town, and most famously Venice. Climate action is on the agenda for cultural districts.

Seattle has developed "light industrial zoning" to encourage retention of crafts such as artisanal cheese-making and glass-making near the city center. Seattle also has three official "cultural districts". This view of a "light industrial zone" shows there is beauty in production of culture too.
Photo: The Boathouse, Seattle, 1994. Photographer: Russell Johnson

Soaring Urban Property Costs

In 2008, for the first time in human history, more than half the world's population lived in cities. Since cities only came to existence 10,000 years ago, we can reasonably ask whether humans are ready to be so urban. Unlike the industrial city, the creative city need not be located near natural resources—it is all about human resources. An unexpected consequence of the ever-densifying urban economy is rising property values. Early indications are that even this pandemic will result only in a slight correction to runaway property prices. Cultural districts play a very important role in the social cohesion and bonding processes so needed in fast-growing cities—especially with increasing migration from the countryside and immigration from other countries. Cultural districts are often formed in low-cost urban areas. As these become fewer and fewer, pressure will increase to privatize those linking spaces between cultural buildings and it may become increasingly challenging to collocate cultural activities and performances in districts at all.

In the future, cultural districts will be expected to do more to combat climate change. This photograph of a protest at the British Museum demonstrates that climate action is at the front steps of museums.

Photo: BP Must Fall, Extinction Rebellion protest outside the British Museum against the climate crisis and colonialism, 2020, Photographer: Andrea Domeniconi © shutterstock.com, all rights reserved

Governance, Equity, and Access

The various elements of a cultural district have different governance structures: some are government line departments; others are independent not-for-profit charitable organizations; theater and artist-run organizations tend to be co-operatives; and there are also for-profit corporations. Then there is the cultural district central authority that needs to coordinate marketing, transportation, infrastructure, security, grounds, and facilities—often in relation to a city or regional entity. Collaboration is challenging at the best of times and even more so when times are difficult.

In the future, we can expect concerns about equity and access such as, for example, the rights of historic neighborhoods versus the needs of racialized, poor, and homeless people to be foregrounded. New forms of governance and regulatory structures need to be created based on principles of equity, caring, and inclusion if cultural districts are to avoid a future of stagnation and irrelevance.

Cultural Districts are Social Constructs

Successful cultural districts are constructed, not born, even though some of their founding members may have been in that location for generations. Cultural districts appear to be physical constructs, but in reality, they are social and economic constructs. This is perhaps the biggest challenge for cultural districts in the future: to deeply understand that they are more than places, spaces, and events.

Cultural districts need the skills and community connections to respond to social change that is constant, continuous, and unexpected. In a world where economies are increasingly driven by the creation of new knowledge, cultural districts should branch out to include scientific, research, and educational organizations. This will create a scene that tips the balance between creative production and consumerism. The leaders of cultural districts will increasingly need to inspire their members to collaborate, to pressure governments to sustain creation, to maintain the public realm, to look outside their disciplines for new partners, and to sustain relationships with communities contributing to their quality of life. Cultural districts have a great opportunity to lead these changes in this historic moment.

1 Leonard Cohen, "Democracy", from the album "The Future", 1992.

2 Daniel Aaron Silver and Terry Nichols Clark, "Scenescapes: How Qualities of Place Shape Social Life", Chicago 2016.

3 Robert Venturi, "Complexity and Contradiction in Architecture", New York 1966.

4 Monika De Frantz, "Tourism Marketing and Urban Politics: Cultural Planning in a European Capital", in: Tourism Geographies, Vol. 20, Issue 3, 2018, pp. 481–503.

5 Gail Dexter Lord and Ngaire Blankenberg (ed.), "Cities, Museums and Soft Power", Washington, D.C., 2016. The Knowledge Quarter was established in the King's Cross area of London in 2014 with thirty-five founding institutions, including existing and new museums, libraries, art centers, theaters, research institutes, media companies, and education organizations. At the time of writing, there are 102 participating organizations.

The GoDown Arts Centre

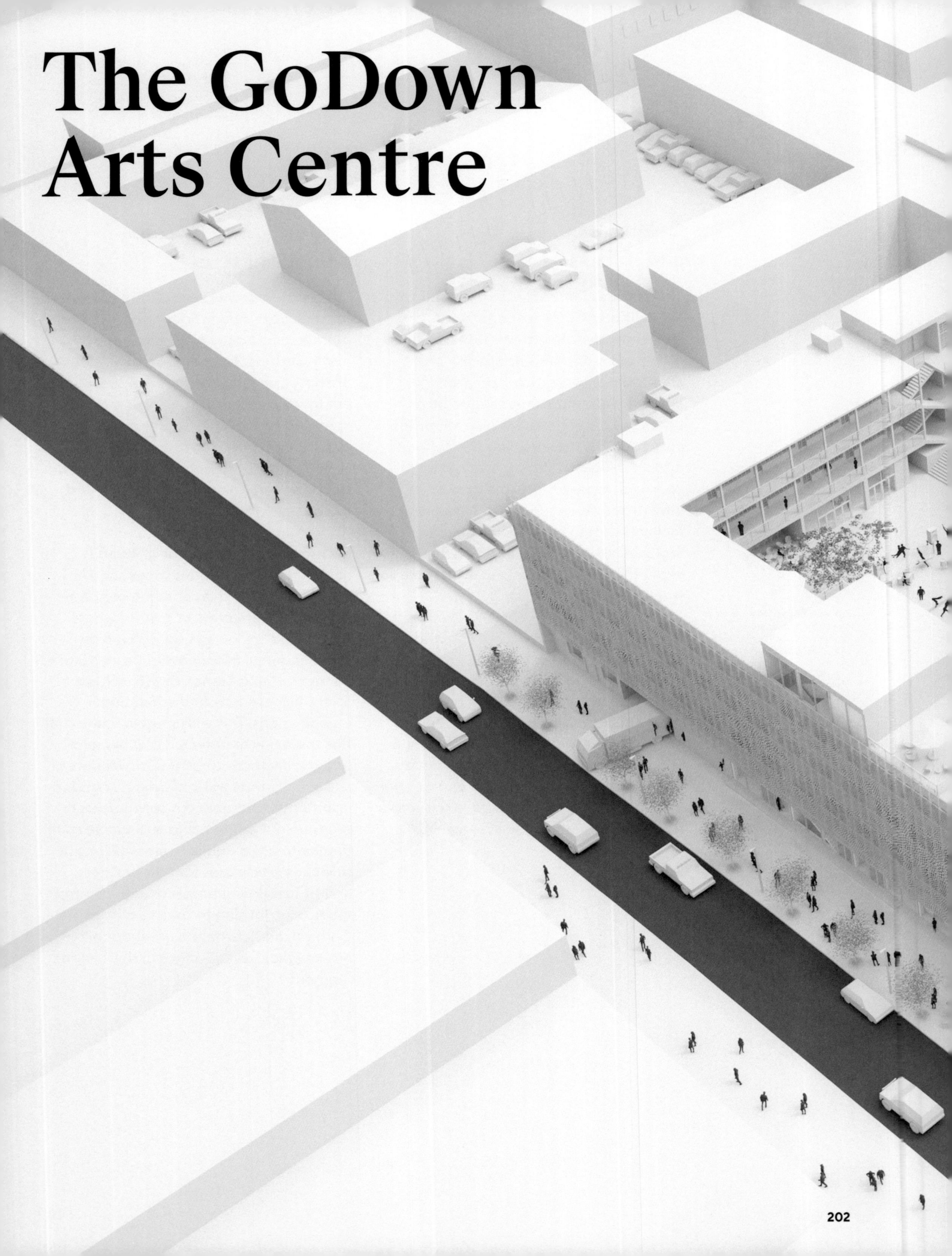

A Cultural Center as Inspiration

by Irene Preißler

As one of the first cultural centers to be established in Africa in the new millennium, The GoDown Arts Centre is a multidisciplinary center for art and culture that provides facilities for artistic expression, from exhibition spaces, galleries, and artist studios to office spaces and rehearsal rooms. The GoDown is a hub for innovation and creativity focused on providing local initiatives with opportunities to realize projects, while also working to strengthen cooperation with regional and international networks.

Location	Nairobi, Kenya, Dunga Rd/Industrial Area (under redevelopment); temporary address: Kayahwe Road, Kilimani
Opened	2003
Total area	1.6 acres (approx. 6,475 m^2)
Number of cultural facilities	approx. 50: artists' studios, performance spaces, museum and art galleries, youth center, children's atelier, training spaces, offices for creative entrepreneurs
Leisure facilities & activities	public open spaces, cafés/restaurants
Visitors/year	100,000–150,000
Architecture	The cultural institutions are mainly housed in former warehouses. New center: White Arkitekter in cooperation with the Kenyan firm Planning Systems Services Ltd.
Website	www.thegodownartscentre.com

History

↑ Lupita—Graffiti of Academy Award-winning actor Lupita Nyong'o, artist: Bankslave
Photo © The GoDown

↖ Previous double page: Rendering of the new GoDown Arts Centre
Photo © White Arkitekter

In 2001, a group of local artists came together with the idea of creating a platform that would support cultural initiatives and artists. They first needed to find a suitable location and considered a variety of spaces, from empty school buildings to warehouses.

In January 2003, they identified a location in Nairobi's Industrial Area. The plot of land belonged to the auto company CMC Motors. The site contained numerous warehouses and depots used for the sale and repair of automobiles and tractors. Once The GoDown Arts Centre took over the space, no time was wasted; artistic projects such as dance workshops were already taking place while the initial structural renovation work was being carried out. The GoDown Arts Centre has since purchased the property from CMC with the help of a grant from the Ford Foundation. The aim was to create not only a space for contemporary art, but also one with which all interest groups could identify. Just nine months after finding the site, in September 2003, The GoDown Arts Centre opened. The name pays homage to the space's original function: in some countries, "godown" is another word for warehouse.

Plans for a new GoDown Arts Centre complex have been under development since 2011, and its completion is planned for 2023.

Architecture

The GoDown Arts Centre was developed on a former industrial site. The original buildings, such as warehouses, were retained and converted into offices and artists' studios.

In 2011, The GoDown Arts Centre launched plans for the construction of a new center on the same plot of land in Industrial Area. The process has been a participatory one, involving the architectural firms White Arkitekter (Sweden) and Planning Systems Services Ltd. (Kenya) and a range of stakeholders including the city government, UN-Habitat (the United Nations Human Settlements Programme), the Kenya Railways Corporation, which is headquartered close to The GoDown, architects, city planners, students, artists, and residents.

The designs by White Arkitekter and Planning Systems Services take account of the ideas and wishes developed jointly in a brainstorming process lasting several years. They see the redevelopment of urban areas as a long-term undertaking that needs to give people scope to develop and adapt the spaces they inhabit to function to suit their ways of living. This process gave rise to a winning design in the Future Projects Category in the World Architecture Festival, 2019.

The GoDown Black Box – Image of The GoDown Auditorium and box office. The graffiti was a collaborative project created by independent artists commissioned by The GoDown
Artists: Bankslave, Point Blank, Swift, and Uhuru
Photo © The GoDown

Nai Ni Who—Festival participants preparing for flag off outside The GoDown
Photo © The GoDown

The new center is based on a three-courtyard layout. The first courtyard has been designed as an entrance and welcome area, surrounded by art galleries, a library, an auditorium, offices, and restaurants. A broad staircase leads to the offices and artists' studios of the second courtyard. The smaller and more intimate third courtyard contains more artists' studios, which are equipped for different artistic disciplines such as fine art, painting, sculpture, and mixed media. Plans also include a boutique hotel, the income from which will help to support the center's cultural programs. Spaces for conferences, training, and workshops are also planned.

The structure of the main building's façade is based on geometric patterns known as fractals, which are found throughout African and Kenyan culture. The resulting permeability of the façade is intended to symbolize the center's spirit of openness and freedom of thought.

The development has also given rise to important partnerships including, but not limited to, the county government, Kenya Polytechnic University College, UN-Habitat, and its Her City project. The partnership with the Kenya Railways Corporation has been particularly significant as its planned Railway City incorporates the territory within which The GoDown sits.

The GoDown Arts Centre is one of the drivers in a new participatory and integrated process that can contribute to a broader, sustainable urban development approach to Nairobi County.

Construction of the new GoDown Arts Centre was originally planned to commence in 2020. However, the COVID-19 pandemic necessitated a delay. Groundbreaking is now planned for 2022 and completion in 2023. The GoDown Arts Centre is currently housed at the temporary Kilimani location until construction is completed.

Organization

The GoDown Arts Centre—incorporated as The Performing and Visual Arts Centre Ltd.—is a non-profit cultural institution and owns its premises. Space at the center is available for artists or cultural initiatives to rent at subsidized rates. All the institutions housed at The GoDown Arts Centre are independent, but occasionally collaborate on projects at their discretion. The site is also used by external artists for presentations, rehearsals, film shoots and other purposes.

The center is managed by a director as well as a voluntary Board of Directors, whose members oversee the various artistic areas. With no public subsidies from local or national government, the center is primarily self-funded through its own income and sponsors.

← Music recording artist Neema Ntalel on stage at The GoDown Gig

→ Kenyan musical group Yunasi on stage at The GoDown Gig

Photos © Paul Kariuki Munene

Structure

The GoDown Arts Centre is easily accessible using public or private transportation, in both cases about a fifteen-minute ride from Nairobi city center. It is located in Industrial Area on a busy pedestrian and vehicular road that connects the surrounding neighborhood with the Central Business District. The temporary Kilimani location is situated in a serene, equally accessible neighborhood where the organization runs a scaled-down selection of activities.

The GoDown Arts Centre is currently open to visitors on weekdays between 9 am and 5 pm.

Programming

Since the arts center opened, it has hosted numerous events, many of which have become staples in Nairobi's cultural calendar.

Artistic activities at The GoDown Arts Centre have taken place on the center's grounds, within other cultural spaces in the city, and in Nairobi neighborhoods and community spaces. These range from visual arts, music, and contemporary dance to discursive formats and entrepreneurship training. Events have been initiated either directly by The GoDown Arts Centre or in cooperation with partners, artists, or cultural initiatives. The objective of these activities is to promote community interventions and encourage dialogue and knowledge exchange between city residents.

The center ran a highly valued artist-in-residence program which gave international artists the opportunity to work on site, participate in training opportunities, and network with fellow artists based at The GoDown Arts Centre and beyond. The GoDown Arts Centre has hosted international exchanges with dance companies from Russia and the United States. The GoDown also currently runs training in creative entrepreneurship and delivers the Copyright X training in partnership with Harvard University and the Berkman Klein Center for Internet & Society at Harvard University. The Creative Entrepreneurship training program has also offered residencies especially to artists from Uganda, Rwanda, Tanzania, and Somalia.

Nubian Exhibition—Photographic exhibition "Kenya's Nubians" by Greg Constantine in partnership with UNHCR portraying the statelessness and denial of citizenship of Nubians in Kenya
Photo © The GoDown

Dance Traffic Week 002—Contemporary Dance Performance "Dance Traffic"—collaboration between Kenyan and Russian contemporary dancers
Photo © The GoDown

These programs have served to bring together a wide variety of interest groups, including creative artists, entrepreneurs, dancers, filmmakers, workers and musicians, making The GoDown Arts Centre a hub of international and local networking, and an important voice in policy-making discussions for the creative sector. In addition to international conferences, the center has hosted numerous community-based workshops, initiatives, and festivals targeting the youth in Nairobi in particular. These include Dunda Mtaani and the annual Nai Ni Who (Who is Nairobi), which was first held in 2013. These festivals have attracted thousands of visitors over the years. They have been an important platform for The GoDown in its role in facilitating community-driven activities and discussions on the future of Nairobi as a city and on the questions of identity and ownership of the spaces people inhabit.

The Nairobi County Art Competition and Exhibition, Manjano, is another important annual event which offers students and practising visual artists a platform to showcase work created in the preceding twelve months, focusing on "Nairobi" as their theme.

In keeping with The GoDown Arts Centre's commitment to offering a safe space for thought-provoking art, the Centre hosted the Kenya Burning initiative, a photographic exhibition of works by both professional photographers and laypersons that addressed the trauma of the violence that followed the 2007 election in Kenya.

This diversity of artistic activity—from creation, to presentation, to communication—generates an atmosphere of creativity for visitors, the institutions, and the artists who live and work at the center.

Impact

Since its inception, The GoDown Arts Centre has evolved into an urban creative hub that meets the needs of artists and the expectations of visitors, and attends to the experiences of area residents. With around three hundred artists working at the site daily and approximately 150,000 visitors annually, The GoDown Arts Centre contributes significantly to the creative economy at county and national level.

Through the Creative Entrepreneurship, Copyright X and other vital trainings, The GoDown Arts Centre has reached an estimated total of nearly 1,000 artists and cultural stakeholders with the aim of equipping them with the skills necessary for a vibrant cultural sector. Furthermore, the trainings offer opportunities for networking and peer learning.

Art and culture have come to be considered essential factors in Kenya's future development and urban planning strategies. "Culture is recognised as the foundation of Kenya's political, economic and social system" (Kenya Constitution 2010).[1]

← Sudanese artist Salah Ammar at work in his studio at The GoDown

→ Kenyan musical artist Juliani on stage during The GoDown's Dunda Mtaani Festival

Photos © The GoDown

In its first phase, The GoDown Arts Centre impacted individual artists and influenced communities to reflect on their spaces and identity. The GoDown is now transitioning into a critical second phase, in which it is expanding as a cultural center and poised to provide new stimulus for its immediate and wider community and thus encourage investment in the expansion of the economy, trade, and tourist infrastructure such as hotels and restaurants.

It is for this reason that the community has been an integral part of the development of the new GoDown Arts Centre from the very beginning. Residents will continue to play an essential role in the cultural activities of the center to strengthen its sense of community and cultural identity.

1 GoDown Transforms Prospectus, p. 7, available at: https://godowntransforms.org/ (last accessed May 26, 2021).

Töölönlahti

The Cultural Transformation of a European Metropolis

by Erwin Uhrmann

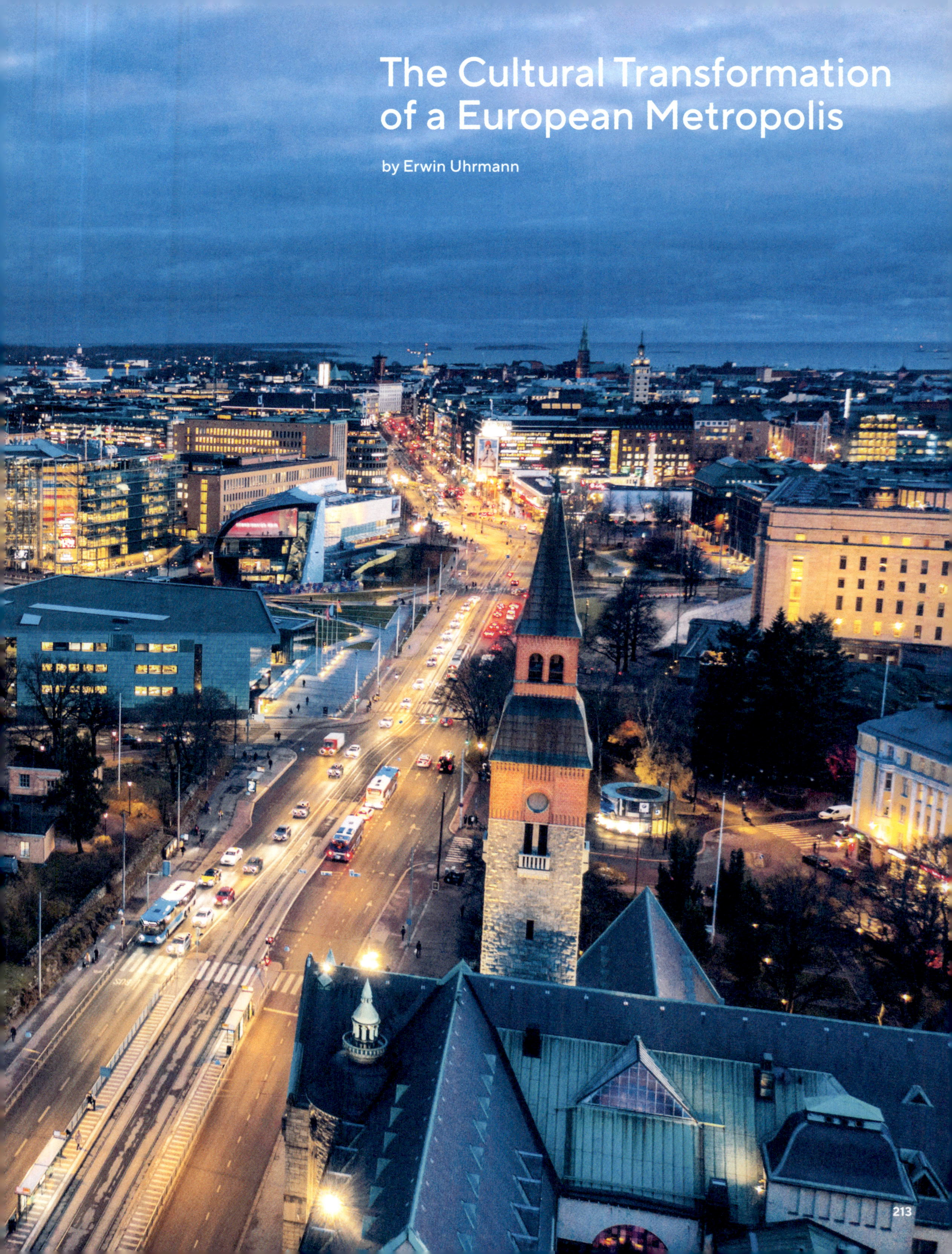

Töölönlahti is a district of Helsinki that stretches from the city center across Töölönlahti Bay to the Olympic Stadium. Over the last 100 years, Töölönlahti has developed into a cultural district where life, art, culture, sport, and nature come together. As Helsinki's center of contemporary culture, it is also a popular gathering place and public space with an ongoing program of festivals and events. In addition to architect Alvar Aalto's Finlandia Hall, Töölönlahti boasts a wealth of other architectural landmarks, arts and cultural institutions, cafés, restaurants, and parks.

Location	Finland, Töölönlahti, Helsinki/adjacent to the city center to the north
Opened	Töölönlahti is a district that has been developing into a leisure and cultural area since the nineteenth century
Total area	110 ha (if the Olympic Stadium area and surroundings are included, the total area is 175 ha)
Number of cultural facilities	8 major institutions in the core area, further institutions in the surrounding area
Leisure facilities & activities	parks, sports fields, playgrounds, and changing recreational activities
Visitors/year (2019)	Museum of Contemporary Art Kiasma: 378,500 Musiikkitalo (Helsinki Music Center): over 1 million Helsinki Central Library Oodi: 3.1 million Villa Hakasalmi: 49,686 Finlandia Hall: 22,000 Opera House: 286,408 Olympic Stadium: 70,000 visitors in August–December 2020 (the stadium was closed for renovation 2016–2020, before that 600,000–700,000 visitors annually) National Museum of Finland: 762,481 Amos Rex Art Museum: 503,700 (autumn 2018–autumn 2019)
Architecture	Villa Hakasalmi (Ernst Lohrmann), Helsinki Central Station (Eliel Saarinen), National Museum of Finland (Hermann Gesellius, Armas Lindgren, Eliel Saarinen), Finnish Parliament (Johan Sigfrid Sirén), Olympic Stadium (Yrjö Lindegren, Toivo Jäntti), Lasipalatsi (Viljo Revell, Heimo Riihimäki, Niilo Kokko), Finlandia Hall (Alvar Aalto), Finnish National Opera and Ballet (Hyvämäki-Karhunen-Parkkinen Architects), Kiasma (Steven Holl), Musiikkitalo (Marko Kivistö, Ola Laiho, Mikko Pulkkinen), Amos Rex (JKMM Architects: Asmo Jaaksi, Freja Ståhlberg-Aalto, Katja Savolainen, Päivi Meuronen), Helsinki Central Library Oodi (ALA Architects: Juho Grönholm, Antti Nousjoki, Janne Teräsvirta, Samuli Woolston)
Website	www.myhelsinki.fi

History & Architecture

Helsinki was not always situated in its present location. Founded by King Gustav Vasa of Sweden at the mouth of the River Vantaa in the mid-sixteenth century, it was moved south to the open sea less than 100 years later to accommodate the docking of large ships. This move allowed Helsinki to compete with the powerful Hanseatic city of Reval (now Tallinn) on the opposite side of the Baltic Sea.

The strong influence of early nineteenth-century Russia is evident in Helsinki's city center. After Helsinki had been destroyed by fire, Czar Alexander I made the city the capital of Finland in 1812 and had it rebuilt in the neoclassical style by the German-Finnish architect Carl Ludwig Engel and the city planner Johan Albrecht Ehrenström. It is to this reconstruction that the city center owes its monumental character.[1]

Töölönlahti, with the Bay of Töölö, was originally connected to the sea via Kluuvi Bay to the south. The area of Helsinki's present center formed gradually over time, especially over the course of the nineteenth century, when Kluuvi Bay was filled in and built up. When the railway arrived in Finland with the opening of the Helsinki-Hämeenlinna line in 1862, Töölönlahti was separated from neighboring Eläintarhanlahti Bay to the east by a railway embankment; the central rail station was built at the bay's southern end.

↖ Previous double page:
Helsinki from above
Photo © Ioannis Koulousis/City of Helsinki

↓ Töölönlahti stretches from the city center across Töölönlahti Bay to the Olympic Stadium, in the foreground Finlandia Hall by architect Alvar Aalto
Photo © Lauri Rotko/City of Helsinki

← The Museum of Contemporary Art Kiasma is one of the many cultural institutions in the Töölönlahti area
Photo © Pirje Mykkänen/Finnish National Gallery

→ The Museum of Contemporary Art Kiasma is designed by American architect Steven Holl
Photo © Susanna Kesänen/Finnish National Gallery

The city grew, and not only in structural terms. The international entrepreneur Henrik Borgström (1799–1883) leased large areas of land from the city, developing them into parks with recreational facilities, bathhouses, and restaurants. Influential city dwellers built villas on the shores of Töölönlahti Bay. One of these is the Villa Hakasalmi, designed in the Empire style by the German architect Ernst Lohrmann for the procurator Carl Johan Walleen, whose stepdaughter Aurora Karamzin sold it to the city of Helsinki. It has been preserved in its original state and is still used by the city as a museum.

In the 1880s, fifteen wooden villas were built on re-zoned land along Linnunlauluntie (Birdsong Road) on the north-eastern side of Töölönlahti Bay, seven of which were removed to make way for traffic planning in the twentieth century. One of the surviving buildings, Villa Kivi, remains available to authors for writing residencies; two other villas are now cafés.

By the end of the nineteenth century, the provision of public spaces for leisure, sport, and recreation had become a key social issue and the subject of much discussion in the Finnish media. After Henrik Borgström's park areas reverted back to the city, the responsible authorities intensified plans to develop the natural areas for recreational

purposes, especially for less privileged people. The gardener Svante Olsson linked several waterfront areas—including Töölönlahti—and planned new parks, with the aim of creating spaces that the people would feel to be "their own".

In 1903, Hesperia Park opened on the southwestern shore of Töölönlahti Bay, replacing the earlier villas and a dense industrial area of factories that had produced sugar, soap, candles, playing cards, and canned foods. The sugar factory in particular had polluted the environment so heavily that even 100 years later, the water in Töölönlahti Bay is still not clean enough for bathing; the area is therefore supplied with clean water via a pipeline from Humallahti.

Finland's independence from Russia in 1917 gave rise to a wave of new ideas and utopian urban planning designs by numerous architects, heralding the Finnish capital's emergence into modernity. Helsinki's first urban planner in this period of awakening was Bertel Jung, whose aim was to reshape the city following the Western model. Together with one of Finland's most influential architects, Eliel Saarinen—who would later emigrate to the USA—he created a plan for the redesign of the city that sought to break down the old hierarchies of urban planning. His design envisaged a radial network of streets running from the suburbs via green zones to a central boulevard leading to the city center. According to this plan, Töölönlahti Bay was to have been filled in. Although the plan was never realized, Saarinen's stamp on the city remains evident in two of his major designs: in 1904, his competition-winning design for the new main railway station produced an architectural icon with neoclassical and art nouveau elements that is still highly regarded today; and between 1905 and 1910, together with his then-partners Armas Lindgren and Herman Gesellius, he built the Finnish National Museum, which likewise features art nouveau elements. Both buildings were built at a time of rapid expansion in Helsinki and continue to characterize the cultural fabric of Töölönlahti to this day.

A further utopian urban design was produced by the architect Johan Sigfrid Sirén, whose 1931 parliament building was built on a hill overlooking Töölönlahti. The decision to build a new parliament coincided with the city's announcement of a planning competition to transform the city center into a modern metropolis. The winner was architect Oiva Kallio, whose design was strongly oriented towards other European cities such as Stockholm. However, the economic crisis and later the Second World War prevented Kallio's plans from ever being realized.

The Olympic Stadium, designed by Yrjö Lindegren and Toivo Jäntti for the planned 1940 Summer Games, was built in the functionalist style between 1934 and 1938 at Töölönlahti's northern end. Due to the Second World War, the games were postponed and finally held in 1952. In 1959, the City of Helsinki again commissioned a new master plan for the city center from architect Alvar Aalto, the Nordic nations' "Father of Modernism". Aalto worked on his plan for over ten years, incorporating different levels into the city structure, with the ground level reserved for pedestrians. Töölönlahti was given a central position. Aalto envisaged a large fan-shaped terraced square at the southern end of the bay and planned a series of public buildings in the Hesperia Park area. Although Aalto created several buildings in Helsinki over the years, his urban master plan was not realized apart from a few exceptions. One of these is Finlandia Hall, built on the west side of Töölönlahti, which was completed in 1971 and extended a few years later. Used for concerts and conferences, the functionalist-style building with its façade of white Carrara marble is one of Helsinki's landmarks. Plans for an opera house had been in the works since the 1920s, but were postponed repeatedly due to a shortage of funds. An architectural competition for an opera house on the Töölönlahti site was tendered in 1975. After numerous delays, the Finnish National Opera, designed by Hyvämäki-Karhunen-Parkkinen Architects, was completed in 1993.

Discussions also arose in the arts sector regarding the construction of a museum for contemporary art. In the mid-1960s, the State Art Commission spoke out in favor of the idea. More and more voices from the art world joined the debate as the need for such an institution grew over the following years and decades, until the museum now known as the Museum of Contemporary Art Kiasma was founded in 1990. At first, Kiasma was temporarily housed in the renovated Ateneum, one of the museums of the Finnish National Gallery, among other locations. In 1992, the American Steven Holl was selected as the winner of an architectural competition to build a new museum; following a construction period of two years, the museum—whose most important building material Holl defines as "Nordic light"—opened in 1998.

The Finnish National Opera and Kiasma were the first new art and cultural facilities in Töölönlahti. The area's development was greatly expanded over the following years and intensified in 2004 through an urban master plan.

The music center and concert hall Musiikkitalo was added in 2011. Designed by the architects Marko Kivistö, Ola Laiho, and Mikko Pulkkinen, the cuboid structure's green copper façade and large glass fronts facing the bay draw a parallel with the nearby Opera House.

The ensemble of cultural buildings around the green Kansalaistori Square was finally completed in 2018 with the opening of the Helsinki Central Library Oodi, designed by ALA Architects (Juho Grönholm, Antti Nousjoki, Janne Teräsvirta, und Samuli Woolston). The bridge-shaped structure is a zero-energy building, constructed primarily of local materials.

Kansalaistori Square and the Makasiinipuisto connect the new cultural buildings and Töölönlahti Bay. Not only does Mannerheimintie Boulevard provide a link between the buildings; an inviting green area where people can linger has been created, too. This cultural axis, along which residential and office buildings were also constructed, extends to Lasipalatsi (Glass Palace), a functionalist building designed by the Finnish architects Viljo Revell, Heimo Riihimäki, and Niilo Kokko. Built in 1936 as a temporary entertainment pavilion for the Olympic Games, it has

↑ JKMM Amos Rex, Lasipalatsi courtyard with the roof and the skylights of Amos Rex exhibition halls (directly underneath the courtyard)
Photo © Mika Huisman/Amos Rex

← Amos Rex, underground lobby

→ Amos Rex Museum is designed by the Finnish Architects JKMM

Photos © Tuomas Uusheimo/Amos Rex

developed into a popular urban meeting place, thanks mainly to the Bio Rex cinema, at one time the largest cinema in Finland. Following extensive redevelopment in the 1990s, the area became a center for culture and media with a host of cafés and restaurants.

With the opening of the privately run Amos Rex Art Museum in 2018, Lasipalatsi gained a new orientation towards the visual arts. Designed by the Finnish architectural firm JKMM Architects (Asmo Jaaksi, Freja Ståhlberg-Aalto, Katja Savolainen, Päivi Meuronen), the museum is located beneath Lasipalatsi's open courtyard. Its roof light openings, constructed as domes with circular skylights and concrete tiles, protrude above the plaza's surface like differently shaped bubbles. Visitors are able to step and climb onto them, which gives the area the feel of a utopian-looking urban landscape and has made it a very popular spot with the public. Amos Rex exhibitions vary from Ancient Egyptian to brand new installation and media art. The collection holds mainly art from the 19th century, but some of the collection is only occasionally on show. The focus is on all kinds of art, regardless of how old it is. The collection originates in the art owned by newspaper publisher and entrepreneur Amos Anderson (1878–1961), whose private collection was housed in another building in Helsinki from the 1960s until 2017.

The combination of these cultural buildings and recreational spaces has given rise to an increasingly cohesive area with lively squares and spacious parks, where the density of culture alternates with the relaxed spaciousness of the natural areas.

Organization

Töölönlahti's art and cultural institutions are independently managed. The City of Helsinki is responsible for the public spaces. In 2017, the city launched an initiative to coordinate cooperation in the district, the result of which was the Töölönlahden kulttuuriverkosto (Töölönlahti Cultural Network), an open network of institutions and organizations active in Töölönlahti that aims to foster cooperation and shared development. Coordinated by the City of Helsinki, the Töölönlahti Network comprises cultural organizations and institutions as well as educational institutions, such as the Sibelius Academy, and business enterprises, all of which exchange information and plan joint events and activities. The network's long-term aims are to increase the area's attractiveness for city residents and visitors, and to bring together culture, leisure, sports, and nature.

Structure

Töölönlahti lies in the immediate vicinity of Helsinki's city center and forms part of a network of public spaces stretching from the central railway station in the south through Kansalaistori Square and the parks around Töölönlahti Bay to Mäntymäki Square and the Olympic Stadium in the north. Töölönlahti is directly surrounded by several interconnected parks and natural areas, including Hesperia Park, Töölönlahti Park, and the Mäntymäki and Kaupunginpuutarha city parks. The surrounding area also includes Makasiinipuisto Park and, above the railway tracks, Kaisaniemi Park. Northwest of Töölönlahti lies Linnanmäki, Finland's oldest amusement park, still considered to be part of Töölönlahti.

Töölönlahti is bordered to the east by the railway embankment, whose tracks lead to the central railway station, and to the west by Mannerheimintie Boulevard. It is impossible to define the area's boundaries precisely, however, due to the constant evolution of the city and its cultural core. Accordingly, Töölönlahti can also be seen to comprise Lasipalatsi and Amos Rex Art Museum and extend as far as Narinkka Square in the Kamppi district in the west and Hakaniemi Market, located slightly further away in the neighboring Eläintarhanlahti Park in the east on the other side of the railway embankment.

The area is large, but close to the city center. All cultural facilities are accessible by public transport.

← Central Library Oodi

→ Central Library Oodi, story room

Photos © Tuomas Uusheimo/City of Helsinki

Programming

Töölönlahti has a high density of cultural institutions, but is also a popular location for leisure, sports, and recreation. The parks contain several children's playgrounds and sports playing fields. The public squares are used for cultural events such as the annual Helsinki Festival, which takes place in the summer in August and September and comprises an extensive range of concerts, film screenings, and other cultural programs, including the use of Kansalaistori Square for the presentation of works of art in the public space. Töölönlahti's mix of cultural offerings includes cultural history, music, literature, and the performing and visual arts. The Finnish National Museum is dedicated to Finland's cultural history from prehistoric times to the present, but also keeps a focus on current affairs through special exhibitions. The Villa Hakasalmi serves as one of Helsinki City Museum's five exhibition venues, featuring changing exhibits on topics related to the city's history, as well as offering the opportunity to experience the historic Empire-style villa itself.

The Museum of Contemporary Art Kiasma, together with the Ateneum Art Museum and the Sinebrychoff Art Museum, forms part of the Finnish National Gallery. Its name, which derives from the Latin "chiasma"—the intersection of two nerves in the body—symbolizes a place of meeting. The museum's focus lies on contemporary art, while the Kiasma Theater serves as a venue for performing arts events, performances, and a wide-ranging educational program.

Amos Rex Art Museum, situated underneath Lasipalatsi, houses with the Amos Rex collection one of the largest private art collections in Finland and focuses mostly on twentieth-century Finnish modern art. It contains 7,000 artworks, mostly paintings, sculptures, drawings, graphics and photographs. The majority of the art pieces were purchased

← Töölönlahti is a popular location for leisure, sports, and recreation.

→ The public squares in the Töölönlahti area are used for many types of cultural events and activities.

Photos © Vesa Laitinen/City of Helsinki

← The Opera House, Auditorium

→ The Opera House

Photos © Heikki Tuuli

after the death of the collector Amos Anderson (1878–1961). The works include pieces by William Lönnberg, Ragnar Ekelund, and Alvar Cawén of the November Group, art from the 1930s and 1940s by Sulho Sipilä and Rabbe and Torger Enckell as well as artists of the Prisma Group, including Yngve Bäck, Sigrid Schaumann, and Sam Vanni. Furthermore, it consists of furniture and other items from Amos Anderson's home. His own collection included a total of 250 paintings and sculptures. About 3–4 exhibitions are held annually. The scope of the Amos Rex exhibitions is vast and varied; they can vary from Japanese video and media art to artefacts from Ancient Egypt and contemporary Finnish art.

The Musiikkitalo (Helsinki Music Center) was built to provide concert facilities acoustically superior to Finlandia Hall, which until then had been used as a multi-purpose event center. The Musiikkitalo is the home of the Helsinki Philharmonic Orchestra, the Finnish Radio Symphony Orchestra, and the Sibelius Academy, which is part of the University of the Arts. Up to 100 events are held every month as part of the Musiikkitalo's own program. The Finnish National Opera and Ballet offers a program of opera and ballet performances from late August to late May or early June. An amphitheater is rented by some societies for dance lessons etc. during the summer.

The Helsinki Central Library Oodi completes the ensemble of cultural facilities on Kansalaistori Square. In addition to its core function as a library, the new building with its visionary architecture serves above all as a comprehensive facility for education in many different formats. It comprises a cinema, recording and photo studios, editing rooms, gaming rooms, an educational kitchen, an immersive smart wall space, and an urban workshop with the newest technology. With every visit, the architecture becomes more and more of an experience in and of itself. The third floor, for example, contains a public balcony, an area for children for various activities. The featured art forms include literature, cinema, digital art, sculpture, music, dance, live performance, gaming, architecture, and design.

Impact

Töölönlahti is an example of how culture can become a key factor in the development of urban areas. Helsinki is strongly influenced by neoclassical and neo-renaissance styles, art nouveau, modernism, and functionalism, and boasts a large number of architectural landmarks. Eliel Saarinen, Alvar Aalto, Viljo Revell and numerous other twentieth-century architects have left their stamp on the cityscape. Helsinki has continued to develop as a cultural oasis in the twenty-first century, especially in Töölönlahti. As a district, Töölönlahti itself is not easy to define. It is home to numerous cultural institutions; within the area's wider radius, however, the number of these institutions increases still further. The Finnish National Theater, the Helsinki City Theater, the Natural History Museum, the Kunsthalle Helsinki, and the Finnish National Gallery are all located only a short distance away.

← The path around Töölönlahti is a popular running track even in the winter time.
Photo © Susa Junnola/City of Helsinki

→ Töölönlahti brings together culture, leisure, sports, and nature.
Photo © Roy Koto/City of Helsinki

↖ Amos Rex, Lasipalatsi Square
Photo © Tuomas Uusheimo/Amos Rex

In addition to the district's parks, Kansalaistori Square is the heart of Töölönlahti; in the twenty-first century, with the Musiikkitalo, Kiasma Art Museum and Helsinki Central Library Oodi, it has developed into Töölönlahti's cultural core, a meeting place, and popular event location. Makasiinipuisto Park, with its sports areas and playgrounds, connects Kansalaistori Square with the bay of Töölönlahti and opens up a whole panorama of local recreational opportunities. Everything is within walking distance; the popular shopping streets flow into the district's cultural heart, and culture merges with nature. Since the beginning of the twentieth century, Helsinki's urban layout has been richly shaped by utopian concepts and ideas. In recent years, the city has also focused on the aspect of sustainability, aiming to become CO_2 neutral by 2035; all projects are being adapted to this end. In addition to ecological sustainability, the factors of well-being, equality, and a functioning social life are also key to the city's strategy for the future.

1 Architecture & Comportement / Architecture & Behavior, Vol. 5, No. 1, 1989, pp. 29–39.

West Kowloon Cultural District

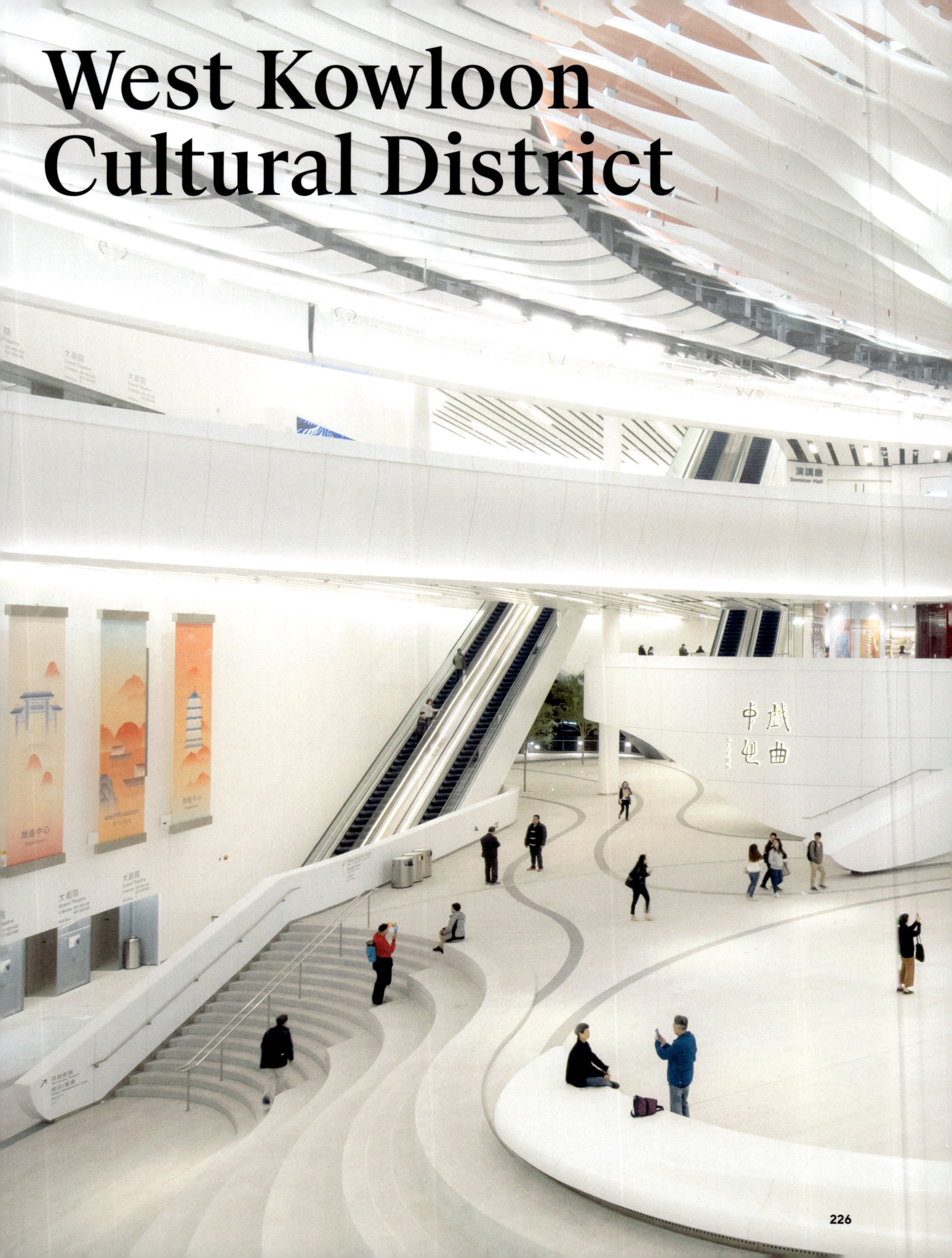

A New Place for Art and Culture

by Irene Preißler

Hong Kong is mainly known as a business and financial metropolis. One of the world's largest cultural quarters, the 40-hectare West Kowloon Cultural District (WKCD or West Kowloon) began major construction in 2013, but has been programming large-scale public events since 2012. Sections of it are already in operation, with other cultural facilities still under construction. With its mix of cultural institutions, the publicly accessible Art Park, educational programs, leisure activities, events, and contemporary architecture, West Kowloon sets new standards for future urban planning.

Location	China, Hong Kong, Austin Road West/ West Kowloon
Opened	2012
Total area	approx. 40 ha
Number of cultural institutions	7 (open or under construction)
Leisure facilities & activities	public open spaces, cafés/restaurants, shops, hotels, office and residential buildings
Visitors/year	n/a, as total area not yet open
Architecture	Foster + Partners, Revery Architecture (formerly Bing Thom Architects) and Ronald Lu & Partners, Herzog & de Meuron together with TFP Farrells and Ove Arup & Partners HK, DLN/West 8/ACLA, Rocco Design Architects, UNStudio/AD+RG, VPANG Architects Ltd. + JET Architecture Inc + Lisa Cheung
Website	www.westkowloon.hk

History and Architecture

This area in the western part of the Kowloon Peninsula was originally reclaimed in the 1990s as part of the infrastructural development for the new Hong Kong International Airport, which included road and rail tunnels that now run under the area, connecting Kowloon to Hong Kong Island.

The idea of establishing a cultural district in West Kowloon was proposed in the then Chief Executive's 1998 policy address. Its goal was to create a vibrant location where the local cultural scene can meet, engage in exchange, and develop.

In 2006, the government appointed the Consultative Committee on the Core Arts and Cultural Facilities of the District to develop the project. Discussions involving the local arts scene also took place. Ultimately, a mix of different cultural facilities was recommended, including theaters of different sizes, a Xiqu (Chinese opera) center, a concert hall, a chamber music hall, a mega-performance venue, a museum, and an exhibition center. At the same time there would be spacious, freely accessible outdoor areas for the general public.

In 2008, the West Kowloon Cultural District Authority (WKCDA) was established and a budget of HK$21.6 billion was approved by the Legislative Council. A three-stage Public Engagement Exercise was conducted between 2009 and 2011, giving the public the opportunity to voice their aspirations and expectations concerning the planning, the three Conceptual Plan Options, and the proposed Development Plan (DP) for the District.

↖ Previous double page: Xiqu Centre atrium

↓ Lyric Theatre Complex (currently under construction)

Photos © Courtesy of the West Kowloon Cultural District Authority

Freespace located in the Art Park
Photo © Courtesy of the West Kowloon Cultural District Authority

In March 2011, the Board of WKCDA announced the selection of City Park, designed by Foster + Partners, as the preferred Conceptual Plan Option on which the DP for WKCD was to be based. "Iconic, world-class and for everyone—this is our mission"[1] is how Norman Foster describes his design, which rests on six principles: innovation, inspiration, highest quality, appealing design, accessibility, and sustainability. Local and traditional as well as international and modern elements have been combined. Art and cultural education are the central focus, but the concept also reflects other aspects of daily life, such as living, working, dining, and shopping. One distinct design feature is the relegation of vehicular traffic underground, forming a large integrated basement, with free movement for people on avenue level.

In order to make the District "a place for everyone", twenty-three hectares of public parks and public open space have been designated for recreation and leisure—an absolute rarity amidst the dense development of the surrounding city. The open spaces will also be used for cultural events and art projects.

Individual facilities are being developed in phases. The Xiqu Centre, the first arts and cultural facility in the district, commenced construction in September 2013 and opened in 2019. Other completed and opened facilities include the M+ Pavilion/Arts Pavilion (2016), Freespace (2019), the Art Park (2019), and the Competition Pavilion (2019). The construction of M+, the first global museum of contemporary visual culture in Asia, has been completed, and this facility is set to open in late 2021.

Other buildings under construction include the Hong Kong Palace Museum, which is planned to open in 2022, and the Lyric Theatre Complex, targeted to open in 2024.

The various facilities all have unique architectural and content concepts corresponding to their positioning. Most venues incorporate catering and shops. They have been conceived to be distributed deliberately throughout the site to produce a natural, organic architectural fabric.

↑ The Competition Pavilion

↓ Lyric Theatre Complex (opening planned for 2024)

Photos © Courtesy of the West Kowloon Cultural District Authority

Organization

West Kowloon Cultural District is a strategic project of the city, intended to position Hong Kong as a cultural metropolis for the future. In 2008, WKCDA was established to fulfil this objective and the West Kowloon Cultural District Authority Ordinance was passed. Accordingly, the WKCDA is bound to the tenets of this Ordinance and reports to the WKCDA Board.

Each cultural institution has its own management team and structure and reports to the WKCDA's Chief Executive Officer. M+ Museum Limited and the Hong Kong Palace Museum Limited are wholly owned subsidiaries of the WKCDA, with their own Boards that report to the WKCDA Board.

This structure gives the institutions creative autonomy. At the same time, they also benefit from the advantages offered by a central organization in areas such as facility management, personnel, ICT, and finance.

↑ Xiqu Centre Grand Theatre

← Xiqu Centre entrance

Photos © Courtesy of the West Kowloon Cultural District Authority

Structure

The Cultural District is situated in a waterfront location in the heart of Hong Kong, overlooking Victoria Harbour and offering views of Hong Kong Island. It is adjacent to Tsim Sha Tsui, one of the most popular shopping and tourist areas in Hong Kong.

When complete it will contain public squares, arts and cultural institutions, shops, restaurants, leisure facilities, and cultural offices. Outdoor areas are publicly accessible around the clock, while the opening hours of the cultural facilities and other institutions vary.

West Kowloon is easily accessible by various means of transport. WKCD is connected to three major railway systems, including the Mass Transit Railway spanning the city, the High Speed Rail connecting Hong Kong with the Mainland's national high-speed rail network, and the Airport Express linking to Hong Kong International Airport. Additionally, once the District is complete a main avenue will connect all its facilities, with the majority of traffic and parking facilities routed underground.

← The Competition Pavilion

→ Waterfront promenade

Photos © Courtesy of the West Kowloon Cultural District Authority

Programming

West Kowloon represents Hong Kong's goal of establishing the city as an international metropolis of art and culture. As an inclusive cultural district, the aim is to provide West Kowloon with high-quality culture, but also to support young talent and creative artists, and to promote both cooperation with creative industries and cultural exchange. At the same time, the intention is not only that there should be an increase in the general population's participation in art and cultural activities, but that a public recreational space be created as well. The objective is to make Hong Kong an even more popular tourist destination and a cultural hub for the entire region.

The district's institutions are dedicated to different cultural genres. Some of them have already been completed, while others are still under construction.

While M+ was still under construction, the M+ Pavilion (opened 2016) served as the space for the first M+ exhibitions at West Kowloon. The design was selected in an open competition won by VPANG Architects Ltd. + JET Architecture Inc + Lisa Cheung.

The Xiqu Centre (opened 2019) showcases traditional Chinese theater and Cantonese opera. It also works to develop these genres further in order to present them to the public in contemporary forms. The building's striking design, conceived by Revery Architecture (formerly Bing Thom Architects) and Ronald Lu & Partners, combines traditional and contemporary elements. It houses the 1,075-seat Grand Theatre, the 200-seat Tea House Theatre, eight studios, and a seminar room. Particularly noteworthy is the Grand Theatre's location on the building's top floor, resulting in the large, covered atrium below with space for exhibitions, performances, and workshops.

Freespace (opened 2019) is Hong Kong's new performance center. Working with national and international artists, the center works to devise new ways of experiencing performances and taking both artists and audiences to their limits. Freespace is divided into The Box, Hong Kong's largest "black box" theater; The Room, a large multi-functional space for exhibits and workshops; The Studio, for meetings, workshops, and small-scale symposiums; and the event venue Livehouse.

With its promenade and view of Victoria Harbour and Hong Kong Island, the Art Park (opened 2019) is West Kowloon's green center, offering space for relaxation and leisure activities as well as large public lawns. There are restaurants and cafés, and two cultural facilities, the Arts Pavilion and Freespace, are also located here. Furthermore, open-air performances, concerts, and other cultural events are regularly held on the lawns.

Situated directly on the promenade, the Competition Pavilion (opened 2019) offers views over the harbor while also providing a space for small-scale events. The building is by the young Hong Kong-based firm New Office Works (Paul Tse and Evelyn Ting), whose design was chosen as the winning entry in an architecture competition held in 2017. Their concept builds upon everyday elements typical of Hong Kong and embeds them in the District's structural fabric. The sloping roof rests on wooden columns that appear to merge with the surrounding trees by virtue of the transparent character of the north and south façades. The pavilion thus also stands as a symbol of the city's diversity. This is a temporary structure and can be relocated to other places in the District.

← Hong Kong Palace Museum (opening 2022)
Rendering © ROCCO Design Architects Limited

→ Art Park
Photo © Courtesy of the West Kowloon Cultural District Authority

The M+ (opening planned for 2021) is dedicated to the visual art of the twentieth and twenty-first centuries, including design, architecture, and the moving image. The aim has been to create a completely new kind of museum, one that reflects a unique time and place. The design by Herzog & de Meuron with TFP Farrels and Ove Arup & Partners HK is based on functionality. Accessible through several entrances, the building's horizontal level comprises thirty-three galleries, three cinemas, a lecture hall, a learning hub, event spaces, a media center, a shop, and a public roof terrace with views of Victoria Harbour and the Hong Kong skyline. Rising vertically from the podium is the Museum Tower, which will house the library, archive, study rooms, offices, and restaurants. The LED façade with a display area of about 110 × 66 m can be used as a canvas for artistic works of moving images. At the same time, the architecture makes deliberate reference to the underground railway line that divides the building, producing a unique atmosphere for exhibitions.

The museum will showcase treasures of the Hong Kong Palace Museum (opening planned for 2022), also known as the "Forbidden City", and present international art using innovative technologies as well as different perspectives, with the intention of strengthening the dialogue between different cultures. Inspired by traditional art and architecture, the design by Rocco Design Architects is a reinterpretation of Chinese aesthetics. In addition to exhibition rooms, the museum will have galleries, interior and exterior relaxation zones, atriums, an auditorium, educational spaces, restaurants, and shops.

Designed by UNStudio/AD+RG, the Lyric Theatre Complex (opening planned for 2024) will showcase the best of Hong Kong and international dance, theater, musicals, and more. A 1,450-seat lyric theater, a 600-seat medium theater, and a 270-seat studio theater are planned. The complex will also house spacious rehearsal rooms and the Resident Company Centre or Dancehouse, where dance companies can work on collaborative projects. It will be a vibrant, creative center for performers and audiences alike.

In addition to its art and cultural facilities and public open space, a total gross floor area of about 500,000 m^2 will be developed in phases for large-scale commercial properties, comprising retail, dining, and entertainment, as well as hotel, office, and residential uses. An approach integrating culture and commerce will be adopted in the commercial master planning. Through a public-private partnership model, WKCDA will invite international developers and investors to realize projects together.

An event at the Competition Pavilion
Photo © Courtesy of the West Kowloon Cultural District Authority

↑ M+, Hong Kong's new museum of visual culture
Photo © Eason Tsang Ka-wai

← Cycling along the West Kowloon waterfront promenade

→ An M+ Pavilion exhibition

Photos © Courtesy of the West Kowloon Cultural District Authority

Impact

Cities are rated as appealing and livable when people aspire to live and work in them, tourists visit them, and their residents take great pride in them. One essential ingredient of this is a varied cultural life. In the past, Hong Kong was known primarily as a financial and business metropolis, but it has seen a vibrant cultural scene emerge in recent years.

West Kowloon lies on the westernmost edge of the Kowloon Peninsula, overlooking the harbor and Hong Kong Island. The project has created an area in which visitors can experience different art forms in one place, and where artists can network and develop joint projects. At the same time, it has also created an area for relaxation right in the middle of the city.

In the adapted version of his original concept, Norman Foster deliberately planned a "limited number of 'star' buildings within the context of more general background buildings and urban spaces, like streets, squares and parks",[2] for "public space is the urban glue that binds the city together, and will be central to the success of the new district".[3] This was borne out by the public's use of the numerous open spaces for various activities when the Freespace Festival was held in West Kowloon for the first time in 2012. Since then, as West Kowloon's green center, the Art Park has become one of Hong Kong's most popular leisure spots. The enlivening of public space with many users and activities remains a fundamental principle, creating a district where culture and leisure co-exist in a fluid and continually evolving relationship.

In this way, West Kowloon contributes subtly yet powerfully to connecting residents with the intangible heritage of their city and setting the course for a sustainable future.

1 https://www.westkowloon.hk/en/the-district/background-142 (last accessed April 17, 2021).

2 Christopher DeWolf, "West Kowloon Cultural District", in: CLADmag, Issue 1, 2015, p. 125.

3 Christopher DeWolf, "West Kowloon Cultural District", in: CLADmag, Issue 1, 2015, p. 125.

The Authors

in the order of their contributions

Christian Strasser

Christian Strasser studied law and business administration. From 1985 to 1999 he was the director of the Linz Posthof, the city's leading venue for contemporary art. During his tenure, his initiatives included the Austrian Cabaret Prize and the Austrian Dance Prize for Contemporary Dance. He also spearheaded the addition of an extension to the center, known as Posthof 2. As procurator of the Ars Electronica Center in its founding year, he contributed to building up the organization and was responsible for its personnel, legal, and finance departments. From 1999 he worked in the real estate and construction sector in Linz, supervising a yearly new construction volume worth between fifty and seventy-five million Euros. Among other projects, he oversaw the reconstruction of Linz Stadium and the extension to the Ars Electronica Center. Christian Strasser was appointed director of the MuseumsQuartier in 2011. Under his direction, the number of visitors has risen continuously.

He was appointed chairman of the supervisory board of Vienna's Burgtheater, leading it through its period of crisis, and continues to serve on supervisory boards in the real estate and cultural sectors.

Louisa Hutton

Louisa Hutton studied at the University of Bristol and the Architectural Association in London, following which she worked with Alison + Peter Smithson for four years. In 1989, Louisa founded Sauerbruch Hutton in London together with Matthias Sauerbruch; since 1993, the agency has been based in Berlin. She taught at the Architectural Association and was a visiting professor at Harvard Graduate School of Design. Louisa was a member of the Curatorial Board of the Schelling Architecture Foundation, and a Commissioner at CABE as well as a member of the first Steering Committee for Germany's Bundesstiftung Baukultur. She is an Honorary Fellow of the American Institute of Architects. In 2014, Louisa was elected to become a Royal Academician, and in 2015, she was awarded an OBE.

Matthias Sauerbruch

Matthias Sauerbruch studied at the Hochschule der Künste Berlin and the Architectural Association School of Architecture in London. He worked at the Office for Metropolitan Architecture (OMA) in London as a project manager for six years and a partner for four years. In 1989 he founded Sauerbruch Hutton together with Louisa

Hutton and has directed the office since then. Matthias taught at the Architectural Association from 1985–1990 as a unit master. He held tenured professorships at the TU Berlin as well as the Academy of Fine Arts Stuttgart between 1995 and 2005. He was a visiting professor at the University of Virginia in Charlottesville (2006), the Harvard Graduate School of Design (2005–2009), as well as the University of the Arts in Berlin (2012–2014). Matthias is a founding member of the German Sustainable Building Council (Deutsche Gesellschaft für Nachhaltiges Bauen), a member of Munich's Urban Design Council, and a board member of the KW Institute for Contemporary Art Berlin. He is an Honorary Fellow of the American Institute of Architects and a member and currently Director of the Architecture Section of the Akademie der Künste, Berlin.

Adrian Ellis

Director, AEA Consulting Chairman, Global Cultural Districts Network
Adrian Ellis is the founder of AEA Consulting (1990) and the GCDN Global Cultural Districts Network (2013), an organization serving those responsible for planning and managing cultural districts globally. He has worked in senior management and as a board member in both museums and the performing arts and as a strategy consultant to leading clients in the cultural sector around the world. Adrian served as Executive Director of Jazz at Lincoln Center from 2007, returning to AEA in 2013.

He has been a Scholar in Residence at Columbia University and a board member of Poets House (New York), All Arts (New York), and the National Museum of Wales. Adrian attended University College, Oxford, where he graduated with an M.A. (First Class) in Politics, Philosophy, and Economics, and also studied at the London School of Economics. His forthcoming book on cultural districts will be published in 2022.

Vitus H. Weh

Vitus H. Weh (*1965) studied applied cultural studies in Hildesheim and lives in Vienna. He works as a freelance exhibition organizer and curator, dramaturg, and scenographer and teaches Museum Studies at the University of Art and Design, Linz. Based on his ideas, the production-oriented Q21 at the MuseumsQuartier Wien (MQ) and the Music City education initiatives at the Vienna Gasometer were established in 2002 and 2014 respectively. He also conceived the nine micro-museums in the public passageways of MQ. They are dedicated to "marginal themes" of museum culture, such as sound art, comics, street art, typography, literature, photography, and sculpture. Since 2013, he has served as contemporary art advisor to the Esterházy Private Foundation in Eisenstadt. He is President of the Kunstverein Eisenstadt, which he and other colleagues founded in 2008.

Gail Lord

Gail Lord is President of Lord Cultural Resources, one of the world's foremost museum planners, a public presenter, and co-author of six museum planning manuals and several books, including "Cities, Museums and Soft Power". Gail co-founded Lord Cultural Resources with her husband Barry Lord in 1981 to provide specialized planning services to museums, the arts, cultural districts, and the creative economy with the goal of making the world a better place through culture. Based in Toronto and New York, Lord Cultural Resources has offices in Mumbai, Dubai, Los Angeles, Madrid, and Beijing. It has completed over 2,500 projects in fifty-seven countries and 450 cities. Gail has been honored as a Member of the Order of Canada and an Officier de l'Ordre des Arts et des Lettres de France, and has received an honorary Doctor of Letters from McMaster University.

Irene Preißler

Irene Preißler has been responsible for Press and Public Relations at the MuseumsQuartier Wien since 2008, supervising its media positioning as an attractive cultural district and leading all communication promoting its extensive program and numerous events. After obtaining a degree in German studies, she embarked on a career in public relations, working for several international companies.

Erwin Uhrmann

Erwin Uhrmann (*1978) lives in Vienna, where he studied communication science and political science at the city's university. He is the author of several novels, poetry collections, and non-fiction books. Between 2011 and 2016 he directed the literature program at the Essl Museum. He is the editor of the "Limbus Lyrik" series, which is dedicated solely to contemporary Austrian poetry. He worked as part of the communications team at the MuseumsQuartier Wien from 2016 to 2021.

Postscript & Acknowledgments

Fifteen cultural districts, fifteen countries, fifteen concepts, an infinite number of ideas; yet all share the same goals: to create added value for visitors, to be open to new ideas, to promote international exchange. And that is precisely what has made it possible to realize a book such as this. Throughout the entire creative process, it has been a great pleasure to collaborate with so many different partners all over the world and to be introduced to new ideas along the way.

As editors of "World Culture Districts—Places of the Twenty-First Century", our team at the MuseumsQuartier Wien would like to thank all those involved for their commitment to realizing this project.

Our thanks go especially to the cultural districts represented in this book; to the directors and staff who, through their work around the world, contribute every day to cultural life and continually set the topics of the future; and to the institutions based at the MuseumsQuartier, whose work has made a significant impact on its history and will play a decisive role in shaping its future.

We also thank the contributors of the essays, who, with their expertise and years of experience in the cultural sector, have illustrated exciting approaches and perspectives.

All of this demonstrates the incredible diversity that makes art and culture so rich and interesting. Let it inspire you, too!

Imprint

World Culture Districts
Places of the 21st Century

Editor
Dr. Christian Strasser, MBA
Director, MuseumsQuartier Wien

Concept & project management
Djeiran Malek-Hofmann, BA, MAS (MQ),
Mag.[a] Irene Preißler (MQ),
Mag. Erwin Uhrmann (MQ)

Editorial team
Djeiran Malek-Hofmann, BA, MAS (MQ),
Mag.[a] Irene Preißler (MQ),
Mag. Erwin Uhrmann (MQ)

Graphic design
Susanna Barborik, Cristina Bianchi (Rosebud)

Fonts
TT Norms
Suisse BP Serif

Copyediting
Margaret Hiley, M. A., Ph. D. (English)
Mag.[a] Pia Praska (German)

Proofreading
Margaret Hiley, M. A., Ph. D. (English)
Dr. Michael Preis (German)

Translation
Dean Kustra (German-English)
Mag. Alexander Moore (English-German)

Published by
VfmK Verlag für moderne Kunst GmbH
Schwedenplatz 2/24, A-1010 Vienna, Austria
hello@vfmk.org
www.vfmk.org

ISBN 978-3-903572-19-5

Printed in Austria
Printed by Holzhausen/Gerin Druck GmbH
Wienerfeldstraße 9, A-2120 Wolkersdorf, Austria

Printed on
Munken Lynx Rough
Magno Volume

Distribution
Europe: LKG, www.lkg-va.de
UK: Cornerhouse Publications,
www.cornerhousepublications.org
USA: D.A.P., www.artbook.com

Bibliographic information of the
German National Library
The German National Library has registered this publication in the German National Bibliography; detailed bibliographic data are available online at dnb.de.

MuseumsQuartier Wien
Museumsplatz 1, A-1070 Vienna, Austria
www.mqw.at